MODERN ASTRONOMY

EXPANDING THE UNIVERSE

Lisa Yount

CHELSEA HOUSE
PUBLISHERS
An imprint of Infobase Publishing

FOR HARRY

who always follows his stars
and has given me a universe of love

MODERN ASTRONOMY: Expanding the Universe
Copyright © 2006 by Lisa Yount

Chelsea House
An imprint of Infobase Publishing
132 West 31st Street
New York NY 10001

Library of Congress Cataloging-in-Publication Data

Yount, Lisa.
    Modern astronomy: expanding the universe / Lisa Yount.
        p. cm.— (Milestone in discovery and invention)
    Includes bibliographical references and index.
    ISBN 0-8160-5746-X (acid-free paper)
    1. Astronomy—History—Popular works. 2. Astronomers—History—Popular works. 3. Astronomy—Technological innovations—History—Popular works. 4. Astronomical instruments—History—Popular works. I. Title. II. Series.
    QB28.Y68 2006
    520'.9—dc22   2005025113

Text design by James Scotto-Lavino
Cover design by Dorothy M. Preston
Illustrations by Sholto Ainslie

Printed in the United States of America

MP FOF 10 9 8 7 6 5 4 3 2 1

This book is printed on acid-free paper.

CONTENTS

PREFACE

The Milestones in Science and Discovery set is based on a simple but powerful idea—that science and technology are not separate from people's daily lives. Rather, they are part of seeking to understand and reshape the world, an activity that virtually defines being human.

More than a million years ago, the ancestors of modern humans began to shape stones into tools that helped them compete with the specialized predators around them. Starting about 35,000 years ago, the modern type of human, *Homo sapiens,* also created elaborate cave paintings and finely crafted art objects, showing that technology had been joined with imagination and language to compose a new and vibrant world of culture. Humans were not only shaping their world but also representing it in art and thinking about its nature and meaning.

Technology is a basic part of that culture. The mythologies of many peoples include a "trickster" figure who upsets the settled order of things and brings forth new creative and destructive possibilities. In many myths, for instance, a trickster such as the Native Americans' Coyote or Raven steals fire from the gods and gives it to human beings. All technology, whether it harnesses fire, electricity, or the energy locked in the heart of atoms or genes, partakes of the double-edged gift of the trickster, providing power to both hurt and heal.

An inventor of technology is often inspired by the discoveries of scientists. Science as we know it today is younger than technology, dating back about 500 years to a period called the Renaissance. During the Renaissance, artists and thinkers began to explore nature systematically, and the first modern scientists, such as Leonardo da Vinci (1452–1519) and Galileo Galilei (1564–1642), used instruments and experiments to develop and test ideas about how objects in the universe behaved. A succession of revolutions followed, often introduced by individual geniuses: Isaac Newton (1643–1727) in mechanics and mathematics, Charles Darwin (1809–82) in biological evolution, Albert Einstein (1879–1955) in relativity and quantum physics, and James Watson (1928–) and Francis Crick (1916–2004) in modern genetics. Today's emerging fields of science and technology, such as genetic engineering, nanotechnology, and artificial intelligence, have their own inspiring leaders.

The fact that particular names such as Newton, Darwin, and Einstein can be so easily associated with these revolutions suggests the importance of the individual in modern science and technology. Each book in this series thus focuses on the lives and achievements of eight to 10 individuals who together have revolutionized an aspect of science or technology. Each book presents a different field: marine science, genetics, astronomy and space science, forensic science, communications technology, robotics, artificial intelligence, and mathematical simulation. Although early pioneers are included where appropriate, the emphasis is generally on researchers who worked in the 20th century or are still working today.

While the biographies in each volume are placed in an order that reflects the flow of the individuals' major achievements, these life stories are often intertwined. The achievements of particular men and women cannot be understood without some knowledge of the times in which they lived, the people with whom they worked, and the developments that preceded their research. Newton famously remarked, "if I have seen further [than others], it is by standing on the shoulders of giants." Each scientist or inventor builds upon—or wrestles with—the work that has come before. Individual scientists and inventors also interact with others in their own laboratories and elsewhere, sometimes even partaking in vast collective efforts, such as when U.S. government and private projects raced, at the end of the 20th century, to complete the description of the human genome. Scientists and inventors affect, and are affected by, economic, political, and social forces as well. The relationship between scientific and technical creativity and developments in social institutions is another important facet of this set.

A number of additional features provide further context for the biographies in these books. Each chapter includes a chronology and suggestions for further reading. In addition, a glossary and a general bibliography (including organizations and Web resources) appear at the end of each book. Several types of sidebars are also used in the text to explore particular aspects of the profiled scientists' and inventors' work:

Connections   Describes the relationship between the featured work and other scientific or technical developments

I Was There   Presents firsthand accounts of discoveries or inventions

Issues   Discusses scientific or ethical issues raised by the discovery or invention

Other Scientists (or Inventors)   Describes other individuals who played an important part in the work being discussed

Parallels   Shows parallel or related discoveries

Social Impact   Suggests how the discovery or invention affects or might affect society and daily life

Solving Problems   Explains how a scientist or inventor dealt with a particular technical problem or challenge

Trends   Presents data or statistics showing how developments in a field changed over time

The hope is that readers will be intrigued and inspired by these stories of the human quest for understanding, exploration, and innovation.

ACKNOWLEDGMENTS

Thanks to the scientists in this book who reviewed their chapters and answered questions and to the many assistants of scientists who patiently conveyed messages and sent (and sometimes re-sent) photographs, permission forms, and other items. My thanks, too, to my editor, Frank K. Darmstadt, for his help and good humor, and to Amy L. Conver, an invaluable copy editor; to my cats, for providing purrs and not knocking the computer off my lap (though they tried); and, above all, to my husband, Harry Henderson, for unending support, love, and everything else that makes life good.

INTRODUCTION

In some ways, astronomy has less direct impact on human life than perhaps any other science. Many astronomers' discoveries involve events that happened billions of years before Earth existed. No breakthrough in this field ever fed a starving child, cured a disease, or stopped a war. But at the same time, perhaps no other science has so profoundly—or repeatedly—changed people's understanding of their place in the universe and the nature of the universe itself.

Astronomy poses many of the same questions that religion does, the deepest questions a human being can ask: What is the universe? How big is it? How did it begin? How will it end? What part do we play in it? Are we alone? Through most of history, in fact, astronomy was part of religion. The astronomers of ancient times usually were priests. They saw the Sun, Moon, and stars as gods or as the homes of gods. They watched the skies to determine the best time to hold religious festivals or to plant or harvest crops.

When astronomy began to change from religion to science in the 16th and 17th centuries, the first astronomers' discoveries contradicted the religious teachings of the time. In 1543, the Polish astronomer Nicolaus Copernicus published a book stating that the Earth was not the center of the universe, circled by the Sun, Moon, and stars, as the church had traditionally taught. Rather, the Earth went around the Sun. Galileo Galilei, an Italian, showed half a century later that some of the "stars" that people had thought of as decorations painted by God on a sort of spherical curtain around the Earth were in fact real bodies that moved and changed over time. Church leaders reacted by imprisoning or even killing some of the scientific upstarts who dared challenge them.

Changing Views of the Universe

Astronomy in the 20th century avoided these painful clashes with religion, but it changed humans' understanding as profoundly as Copernicus and Galileo did. At the start of the century, soon after George Ellery Hale, the first astronomer covered in this book, built his first large telescope, people thought the solar system was essentially at the center of the universe, much as people of Copernicus's time had believed the Earth was. Astronomers in the early 1900s knew that the Sun was just one star among many in the Milky Way galaxy, but they assumed that it was the only star with planets—let alone a planet bearing intelligent life. Similarly, most thought that the Milky Way was the only galaxy in the universe. They were also confident that, although planets and stars might move, the universe as a whole did not really change over time.

By the end of the century, that picture had altered completely. Astronomers had shown that the Sun is a rather average star, located on one of the Milky Way's spiral arms rather than in the galaxy's center. The solar system is one of an untold number of planetary systems. Similarly, the Milky Way is just one among billions of galaxies. Those galaxies, in turn, are mere specks compared to vast masses of invisible, or "dark," matter surrounding them, whose nature is completely unknown.

Far from being unchanging, astronomers now believe, the universe began in a tremendous explosion and has been flying apart ever since. Indeed, thanks to a strange force called dark energy, the galaxies are fleeing from one another today at an ever-increasing rate. Matter seems doomed to be spread more and more thinly through expanding space, until essentially nothing is left—unless, as some believe, the universe someday reverses itself and begins contracting, ultimately starting the whole cycle of creation over again. As astrophysicist Robert Kirshner wrote in his book about dark energy, *The Extravagant Universe,* "The universe is wilder than we imagine: We keep underestimating how weird it really is." Indeed, even the idea that there is only one universe may someday seem as outmoded as belief in a single solar system or a single galaxy seems today.

Although many astronomers and physicists contributed to the revolution in understanding time and space that took place during the 20th century, the 12 men and women profiled in this volume of the Milestones in Discovery and Invention set, *Modern Astronomy: Expanding the Universe,* were leaders in bringing about this change. Edwin Hubble, for example, showed that the Milky Way was one galaxy among many in a universe that, for unknown reasons, was constantly growing larger. George Gamow proposed that the expansion began with the cosmic explosion that others later termed the *big bang.* Geoffrey Marcy, Paul Butler, and their fellow planet hunters demonstrated that the Milky Way galaxy (and probably other galaxies too) contains many planets, and Frank Drake made people take seriously the possibility that some of those planets might harbor intelligent civilizations. Vera Rubin showed that at least 90 percent of the matter in the universe was, and probably always would be, invisible to any kind of telescope. Saul Perlmutter, Brian Schmidt, and their coworkers offered convincing evidence that the effects of all matter put together, including the dark matter Rubin had discovered, are dwarfed by the power of the even more mysterious dark energy.

A Three-Way Dance

Just as important as the theorists who propose new views of the universe, such as Gamow, and the observers who test them, such as Rubin, are the inventors who create new tools for the observers to use. Astronomy, like other sciences, moves forward in a three-way dance of theory, observation, and technology. Theorists make predictions that observers test. If the needed observations cannot be made with existing technology, observers design, inspire, or borrow something new. New technology, in turn, often produces observations that no theory could have predicted. Theorists revise their ideas to account for what observers report, make new predictions—and the dance continues.

The dance has been under way since the beginning of scientific astronomy. Copernicus's theories were simply speculations until Galileo, observing with a newly invented device called a telescope, provided evidence to support them. As larger and better telescopes were built in the following centuries, they made more discoveries possible, such as William Herschel's finding of the planet Uranus in 1781. These observations spawned revised theories and predictions. For instance, British astronomer John Couch Adams and French mathematician Urbain-Jean-Joseph Le Verrier noticed that Uranus did not quite follow the path that would have been expected from Isaac Newton's laws of gravity. They predicted that a still more distant planet would be found to be pulling Uranus slightly out of its orbit. In 1846, two astronomers, Johann Gottfried Galle and Heinrich-Louis d'Arrest, looked at the part of the sky pinpointed by Couch and Le Verrier and spotted the planet Neptune for the first time.

Improved telescopes were not the only new technology that led to advances in astronomy. In 1835, for example, the French philosopher Auguste Comte declared that scientists would never be able to learn the chemical composition of stars—but, in fact, a device that would let astronomers do just that had already been invented. Isaac Newton had shown in 1666 that when sunlight passes through a triangular piece of glass, called a prism, a rainbow of colors is produced. Newton recognized that this *spectrum,* as he termed it, appears because white light is made up of rays of different colors that the prism bends, or refracts, to different degrees. In 1815, Joseph von Fraunhofer, a German telescope maker, passed sunlight through a vertical slit, then through a lens, a prism, and, finally, a small telescope. This arrangement produced a spectrum in the form of colored lines rather than the continuous rainbow Newton had seen. Later, in 1859, German scientists Gustav Kirchoff and Robert Bunsen showed how to use Fraunhofer's device, the spectroscope, to identify different chemical elements on Earth or in the Sun and other stars.

Advances in technology have also powered the achievements of 20th-century astronomy, and several of the people profiled in *Expanding the Universe* created or championed new devices that let astronomers observe in ways that had never been possible before. Grote Reber took observation beyond light for the first time, showing that the longer waves of radiation called radio waves could also be used to form images of the sky. Riccardo Giacconi carried observation into X-rays, a form of radiation with very short wavelengths. Lyman Spitzer took telescopes into space, where they could form images undistorted by Earth's shimmering atmosphere and capture forms of radiation that the atmosphere blocks out.

The interplay of theory, observation, and technology begun in the time of Copernicus and Galileo has continued in modern astronomy. George Ellery Hale's turn-of-the-century telescopes, bigger and better than any ever built before, let Edwin Hubble make the observations that revealed distant galaxies and the expansion of the universe. Hubble's discoveries, combined with Albert Einstein's theory of relativity, led to George Gamow's theory about the "big bang," the sudden expansion that began the universe. Grote Reber's development of radio astronomy made possible the discovery of cosmic background radiation, the most important evidence supporting the big bang theory. Frank Drake's search for signals from civilizations in other solar systems also used radio astronomy. Drake's hunt, in turn, helped inspire Paul Butler and Geoffrey Marcy's pursuit for physical evidence of extrasolar planets. Vera Rubin used Hale's Palomar telescope to make some of the observations that unveiled dark matter, and other astronomers obtained early information about this mysterious substance from Riccardo Giacconi's X-ray telescopes. Saul Perlmutter and Brian Schmidt used Lyman Spitzer's space telescope in the studies of exploding stars that led them to the discovery of dark energy.

The dance of theory, observation, and technological advance is sure to continue. Theorists are beginning to speak of multiple universes and dimensions, as well as types of matter and energy unknown to present-day physics. Observers are planning programs to capture the light of stars and galaxies born not long after the universe itself. Engineers and space scientists are designing new generations of telescopes on Earth and in space, new devices to collect and record all forms of radiation more sensitively than ever before, and new computer software to analyze what the devices detect.

A hundred years from now, scientists are likely to have revealed a universe as different from the one imagined today as ours is different from the one pictured in Hale's time. As Vera Rubin wrote in the June 2003 issue of *Astronomy*, "Astronomy has an exciting, perhaps endless, future"—a future fueled by the same awe and wonder that humans have felt, since the beginning of their existence, whenever they looked up at the night sky.

1

MORE LIGHT

GEORGE ELLERY HALE AND LARGE OPTICAL TELESCOPES

As the 19th century neared its end, astronomy seemed to be ending as well—and at the same time reaching toward a new beginning. New devices were letting astronomers discover facts, such as the chemical makeup of distant stars, which they had thought were beyond the grasp of science. Yet at the same time, astronomers' classic tool, the telescope, appeared to be reaching its limit.

The telescope that William Parsons, the third earl of Rosse, built on his Irish estate in 1845 provided one example of these limitations. Rosse's telescope rose 56 feet (17 m) into the air and had a main mirror that was 72 inches (1.8 m) across. It was no wonder that people nicknamed the telescope, which weighed three tons (2.72 metric tons), the Leviathan, after a gigantic sea monster in the

George Ellery Hale oversaw the building of three of the world's largest telescopes in the early 20th century. He was also a pioneer solar astronomer and the first astrophysicist. (Yerkes Observatory photograph)

1

Bible. Rosse's Leviathan was a reflecting telescope (reflector for short), which meant that it used a large mirror to gather light. The mirror in a reflector focuses light on a smaller mirror, which in turn sends the light to the observer's eye. In Rosse's day, mirrors were made of metal. They were hard to shape, and they tarnished easily. These problems, plus the fact that big telescopes were very difficult to turn, made reflectors much larger than the Leviathan seem impractical.

Refractors, the other major kind of telescope (and the first kind to be invented), also appeared to have become about as big as they could be. Refracting telescopes use lenses instead of mirrors to focus light. The larger a telescope lens is, the thicker it must be—and the thicker it is, the more light it will block. In addition, unlike a reflector's main mirror, a refractor's main lens must be at the top of a tube, supported only at the edges. Because lenses are made of glass, a kind of liquid, gravity may make a large lens sag in the middle, ruining its power to focus light. In 1888, Lick Observatory in northern California completed what was then the largest refractor in the world, with a lens 36 inches (0.9 m) wide. Most astronomers thought that lenses much bigger than this would be too thick and heavy to be useful.

New Tools for Astronomy

Just when telescopes seemed unable to grow any further, two new tools enhanced their power beyond anything that earlier astronomers could have imagined. At the same time, these tools—the camera and the spectroscope—greatly increased the need for telescopes that could gather more light than existing ones.

In 1840, 14 years after photography was invented, American chemist Henry Draper took the first astronomical photo, a picture of the Moon. Astronomers quickly realized how much photography could help them. Photographs produced a permanent record that scientists could measure, study repeatedly, and share. Furthermore, a camera attached to a movable telescope, set to follow a star across the sky, could gather light from the star for minutes or even hours. As a result, objects too faint to be seen directly through a telescope appeared as if by magic on photographic plates. To obtain enough light and focus it sharply enough to produce clear pictures of dim objects, however, astronomers needed bigger and better telescopes.

Spectroscopes were equally valuable, providing a sort of rainbow bar code that told astronomers what chemical elements a star contained. Each element had its own pattern of dark or colored lines. Adding a camera to a spectroscope allowed the stars' spectra (plural of spectrum) to be photographed. The photographs, however, were often faint and blurry, and the lines in the spectra were too close together to be analyzed easily. Larger, more accurate telescopes could help to solve these problems.

Teen Astronomer

As the 19th century faded and the 20th began, one man gave astronomers telescopes with the greater light-gathering power they needed. This man, George Ellery Hale, made significant advances in his own astronomical field, the study of the Sun. He is most remembered, however, for having brought into existence three telescopes that, in his time, were the largest in the world. They are still among Earth's biggest optical telescopes, or telescopes that view the universe by means of visible light.

Hale was born in Chicago on June 29, 1868, to William E. and Mary Hale. William Hale was a struggling engineer and salesman at the time George was born. During George's childhood, however, William made a fortune building elevators for the new skyscrapers that replaced buildings destroyed in the Great Chicago Fire of 1871.

George was a sickly child, and his worried parents lavished him with attention and care. When he showed an interest in science, his father bought him any scientific instrument that took the boy's fancy. George wanted microscopes at first, but when a neighbor introduced him to astronomy during his teenage years, telescopes and spectroscopes took over. William Hale bought George a used four-inch (10-cm) refracting telescope (the measurement refers to the diameter of the opening at the telescope's light-gathering end). George mounted it on the roof of his family's home and used it to study the Sun.

Student Inventor

George Hale began studying mathematics, physics, and chemistry at the Massachusetts Institute of Technology (MIT) in Cambridge in 1886. The university offered no courses in astronomy, so Hale continued learning that subject by volunteering at the nearby Harvard College Observatory.

Even before Hale graduated from MIT, he invented a major new tool for observing the Sun. This device, the spectroheliograph, moved an image of the Sun slowly past a spectroscope with a narrow slit that admitted only one color of light, corresponding to one chemical element. The result was an image of the Sun in terms of only that element.

Hale built his first spectroheliograph in 1889. He and Edward C. Pickering, the Harvard College Observatory's director, proved its value in April 1890 by photographing the spectra of solar prominences, huge clouds of glowing gas that erupt from the Sun's surface, in daylight for the first time. Solar astronomers hailed the spectroheliograph as an important advance, and it is still considered a basic tool for this branch of astronomy.

Pioneer Astrophysicist

George Hale graduated from MIT with a bachelor's degree in physics in June 1890. Two days later, he married Evelina Conklin, a young woman he had known since he was 13 years old. The pair moved into the Hale family home in Chicago, and Hale, funded by his ever-cooperative father, set up a small professional observatory there. This facility, which Hale called the Kenwood Physical Observatory, was legally incorporated by the state of Illinois in 1891. It contained a 12-inch (30-cm) refracting telescope as well as a spectroheliograph and other instruments.

William Rainey Harper, the young president of the new University of Chicago, was eager to obtain the services of both George Hale and his observatory. Harper offered Hale a position on the faculty if Hale would donate the Kenwood instruments to the university. Hale rejected the offer in 1891, but in 1892, impressed with the quality of other scientists the university had hired, he changed his mind. Hale's father agreed to give the university the Kenwood Physical Observatory and instruments if the university would promise to build a large observatory for Hale two years from the time the young man joined the faculty.

Harper and the university trustees agreed to William Hale's proposal, and on July 26, 1892, George Ellery Hale joined the University of Chicago as the world's first professor of astrophysics. An astrophysicist studies the physical and chemical characteristics of astronomical objects and phenomena. In a biographical note quoted by Florence Kelleher, George Hale later wrote, "I was born an experimentalist, and I was bound to find the way of combining physics and chemistry with astronomy."

Thrilling Pieces of Glass

Later that summer, a chance conversation set George Hale on the path to acquiring what would become the centerpiece of his observatory-to-be. During a chat after dinner at a meeting of the American Association for the Advancement of Science in Rochester, New York, Hale heard renowned optician Alvan G. Clark describe two 42-inch (1.07-m) glass disks sitting in Clark's shop in Cambridgeport, Massachusetts. The University of Southern California (USC) had intended the disks to become lenses for a refracting telescope to be set up in a new observatory on Wilson's Peak, in the San Gabriel Mountains 10 miles (16 km) northeast of the city of Pasadena. The university, however, had run out of money before the observatory or the telescope could be built.

Hale realized that a telescope with lenses this size would be the largest refractor in the world. He rushed back to Chicago to tell his father about the thrilling pieces of glass. William Hale shared his son's excitement, but even he could not afford to buy the disks, have them ground into lenses, and build a telescope around them. For the first—but far from the last—time, George Hale had to turn

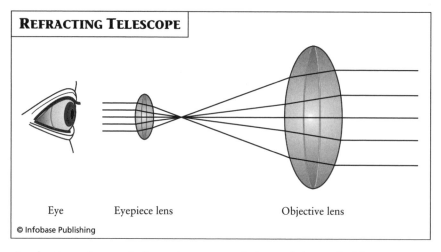

REFRACTING TELESCOPE

Eye   Eyepiece lens   Objective lens

© Infobase Publishing

A refracting telescope (refractor) uses curved pieces of glass called lenses to bend, or refract, light and focus it on a single point.

from astrophysics to fund-raising in order to obtain the telescope he wanted. Fortunately for astronomy, he proved as skilled at the second activity as he was at the first.

Building an Observatory

After several months of searching, Hale found someone willing to build his telescope. The donor was Charles Tyson Yerkes, a wealthy businessman who had developed Chicago's elevated streetcar system. Yerkes's bank account was more impressive than his reputation (he had been arrested for embezzlement in his earlier years), and the city's social leaders refused to accept him. Hale and William Harper persuaded Yerkes that a prestigious astronomical observatory bearing his name would bring him the status for which he longed. In October 1892, the streetcar baron agreed to give the University of Chicago $1 million to build an observatory at Williams Bay, Wisconsin, an easy train ride from Chicago.

While the observatory was being constructed, Hale's career was prospering. He won the Janssen Medal, the French Academy of Sciences' highest astronomical award, in 1894. In 1895, he proved that the element helium, previously detected only in the Sun (by means of spectroscopes), also existed on Earth. Hale later won the Henry Draper Medal of the National Academy of Sciences (1904), the Catherine Bruce Medal of the Astronomical Society of the Pacific (1916), the Copley Medal of Britain's Royal Society (1932), and numerous other scientific medals and awards.

The 40-inch (1.02-m) refracting telescope containing Clark's lenses, mounted in a tube 63 feet (19 m) long, was completed in May 1897. It is still the largest refractor in the world. The Yerkes Observatory was dedicated on October 21, 1897, and Hale, only 29 years old, became its first director. Astronomers

The 40-inch (1.02-m) Yerkes Observatory refractor is the world's largest refracting telescope. (Yerkes Observatory photograph EIB6551)

immediately recognized the observatory, which also contained several smaller telescopes, spectroscopes, and other instruments, as the world's best astrophysical laboratory.

From Refractors to Reflectors

In the late 1890s, George Hale worked in his new observatory to compare the spectrum of the Sun with those of other stars. Making these comparisons stirred his interest in the way stars change during

I WAS THERE: A NEAR-DISASTER

Several astronomers, including George Hale, used the great Yerkes refractor for the first time on the night of May 28, 1897. They raised the movable floor around the telescope to its highest point so they could see through the instrument's eyepiece. One scientist heard a strange noise as they did so, but they could find no cause for it. When they went home at about 3 A.M., they left the floor up because a contractor was supposed to work underneath it the next day.

Helen Wright recounts in her biography of George Hale that just as the contractor, J. C. McKee, arrived at the observatory a few hours later, he heard a terrible crash:

> He ran to the dome, climbed up on a windowsill, and peered through the window. The huge rising floor lay in ruins under the great telescope. McKee clambered down and ran to Hale's house. Hale leaped out of bed, threw on a robe, and dashed to the observatory. Soon [E. E.] Barnard [one of the astronomers] arrived. Together they gazed in silence at the ruin in the dome pit. . . . "It looked," said a man from the Chicago Tribune [shortly afterward] "as if a cyclone had slipped through the slit and gone on a rampage."

Two of the cables that held up the floor apparently had broken, making the floor fall down on one side. If the cables had given way a few hours earlier or later, either astronomers or construction workers surely would have been killed.

Hale and others had to wait until mid-August, after the floor was finally repaired, to learn whether the crash had damaged the big telescope lens. When the group finally looked through the telescope, William Sheehan and Dan Koehler quote E. E. Barnard as saying, "To our consternation, there was a great, long flare of light running through every bright star we examined." Such a flare suggested that the lens had cracked.

Fortunately, when Hale examined the lens itself the next day, he found the true cause of the flare. "During the time the tube remained at rest, while the new floor was being put in, a solitary spider had crawled up the great telescope in the direction of the light," Barnard wrote. "As the days went by and he slowly starved to death, he spun his web." Once the spiderweb was removed, the view through the telescope was perfect.

their lives. To explore this subject further, he knew he would need spectra sharper and more spread out than even the Yerkes refractor could produce.

Never satisfied with the instruments he had, Hale always looked toward better ones. Helen Wright says, in her biography of Hale, *Explorer of the Universe,* that "More light!" was this pioneer astronomer's constant cry—and Hale, like most other astronomers of his time, realized that obtaining more light meant turning from refractors to reflectors.

Unlike the lenses of refractors, the mirrors of reflecting telescopes could focus all colors of light correctly. By the turn of the century, furthermore, improved mirror technology made possible the building of reflectors far bigger and better than Rosse's Leviathan. Instead of being made of metal, mirrors were created by spraying a sheet of glass with a thin, smooth film of silver or other liquefied metal. Glass mirrors were easier to make than metal ones, and they did not tarnish.

After only a few years at Yerkes, George Hale began to think about building a large reflecting telescope. Anticipating him, Hale's father had purchased a 60-inch (1.5-m) glass disk in 1894 and had it delivered to the Yerkes Observatory. At that time, William Hale

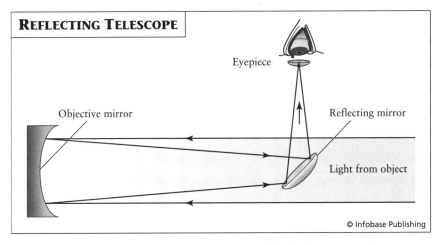

A reflecting telescope (reflector) uses mirrors to reflect light in a way that focuses it on a single point.

had said he would donate the disk to the University of Chicago if the trustees would build a second observatory to house it. The university had no money for such a facility, however, and Charles Yerkes refused to give any more.

A Difficult Climb

Once again, George Hale had to find someone to fund his dream. He spotted a possibility on January 10, 1902, when he read a newspaper article stating that steel magnate Andrew Carnegie was donating $10 million to establish a philanthropic organization for the support of scientific research. Two weeks after Hale saw the article, he sent a letter describing his proposed telescope and observatory to the new Carnegie Institution's executive committee.

Hale wanted to build the observatory on Wilson's Peak (by then called Mount Wilson), the site that the University of Southern California had abandoned. He thought California's warm weather and clear skies would be good for both astronomy and his daughter, Margaret, who suffered from asthma. In June 1903, before the Carnegie committee had voted on his proposal, Hale went to California to see the mountain for himself. At the time, the only way to reach the top of Mount Wilson was to ride up on the back of a burro, but Hale, who had always been fond of the outdoors, enjoyed the adventure.

Hale concluded that the Mount Wilson Observatory site was everything he had hoped it would be. He also liked Pasadena, the city nearest to the mountain. Optimistically, he sent his family to California in October 1903. He returned there himself in December, even though he had just learned that the Carnegie Institution had turned him down.

Mount Wilson Develops

In early 1904, Hale set up a small solar research station on Mount Wilson and began doing research there. He also reapplied to the Carnegie Institution, and this time his optimism was better placed.

The institution granted him $10,000 in April and promised to consider giving him a larger amount in December.

Encouraged, Hale signed a 99-year lease with the company that owned the land on Mount Wilson and started construction of a dormitory for the astronomers who would use the observatory. All the supplies for building the dormitory, and later the observatory as well, were hauled up the mountain by burros and mules. The dormitory came to be known as "the Monastery" because women were not allowed to stay there; Hale and the Carnegie Institution assumed that all visiting astronomers would be men.

As usual, Hale was working ahead of his funding. He was greatly relieved, therefore, when he learned on December 20 that the Carnegie committee had voted to give him $300,000 for the new observatory. He resigned as director of Yerkes on January 7, 1905, and became the director of the proposed observatory on Mount Wilson instead.

Hale pictured Mount Wilson chiefly as a facility for studying the Sun and, secondarily, for learning about how stars developed. The first telescope set up at the observatory was the Snow solar telescope, which Hale and others began to use in 1905. For many years, Mount Wilson was considered the best solar observatory in the world. In 2006, the observatory is still keeping the longest continuously running record of the Sun's activity.

The Mount Wilson Observatory soon attracted astronomers who studied the night sky as well. It came to house not only the 60-inch (1.5-m) reflector, completed in 1908, but also the Hooker Telescope, a reflecting telescope with a 100-inch (2.5-m) primary mirror. This telescope was named after John D. Hooker, a Los Angeles businessman whom Hale, with his usual skill, had persuaded to donate the money for the mirror; the Carnegie Institution paid for the telescope itself. Finished in 1917, this telescope became the showpiece of the Mount Wilson Observatory, just as the 40-inch (1.02-m) refractor was for Yerkes. The Hooker Telescope was the biggest telescope in the world for 30 years—until George Hale's next project replaced it. Although growing light and air pollution from the Los Angeles area have made some of its telescopes less useful than they were in Hale's time, Mount Wilson is still an important observatory.

Sunspotting

George Hale carried out important solar research at Mount Wilson; for example, he took the world's first photographs of a sunspot spectrum there in 1905. Sunspots are dark patches on the Sun's surface. They had been shown to appear and disappear in an 11-year cycle, but no one knew much else about them. Hale found that sunspot spectra

The 200-inch (5.08-m) Hale Telescope at the Mount Palomar Observatory in California was the largest optical telescope in the world until the 1970s. (Dr. T. H. Jarrett, Caltech)

TRENDS: BIGGER AND BETTER TELESCOPES

Each of George Ellery Hale's telescopes was bigger and better than the one before. A telescope's light-gathering power increases as the square of its diameter. This means that doubling the diameter of a telescope mirror makes the telescope able to gather four times as much light, not twice as much. Here are the light-gathering abilities of Hale's four telescopes.

Telescope	Size of mirror or lens	Light-gathering power compared to human eye
Yerkes refractor	40 inches (1.02 m)	35,000 times as great
Mount Wilson smaller reflector	60 inches (1.5 m)	57,600 times as great
Hooker reflector	100 inches (2.5 m)	160,000 times as great
Hale reflector	200 inches (5.1 m)	640,000 times as great

resembled laboratory spectra made at low temperatures. He therefore concluded that sunspots were cooler than the rest of the solar disc.

In 1908, continuing his sunspot studies, Hale made the most important discovery of his scientific career. After noticing that some lines in the spectra of sunspots were split, he theorized that the splitting was caused by a phenomenon called the Zeeman effect, which makes divided lines in spectra when the light creating the spectra passes through a strong magnetic field. If this was true, Hale concluded, sunspots must contain powerful magnetic fields. He and another scientist, Arthur S. King, confirmed his theory by using a powerful electromagnet to duplicate the divided sunspot spectra in the laboratory. Hale later saw swirling clouds of hydrogen near sunspots and guessed that these hydrogen storms produced the magnetic fields.

The Biggest Telescope of All

Exhaustion, depression, and growing signs of mental illness led George Hale to resign as director of Mount Wilson in 1922. He continued to work at his private solar laboratory in Pasadena, however, and by the late 1920s, he was once again planning a new observatory with a telescope that would gather more light than any other had done. This dream telescope would have a primary mirror 200 inches (5.1 m) across, twice the size of the mirror in the Hooker Telescope.

Hale persuaded the California Institute of Technology (Caltech) in Pasadena, a facility he had helped to develop, to return the favor by supporting his plans. As with his other observatories, however, he had to find most of his funding outside the university community. This time, the Rockefeller Foundation provided the $6.5 million that the undertaking would require. For once, however, Hale did not have to beg for the money. In 1928, after reading a *Harper's Magazine* article by Hale that included a plea for a donor to fund a large telescope, Rockefeller's International Education Board contacted him with their offer.

City lights in the Los Angeles basin were already starting to make some types of observation difficult on Mount Wilson, so Hale wanted his new project located much farther from civilization. In 1934, he chose 5,600-foot (1,697-m) Mount Palomar, near San Diego, California, as his site. San Diego, about 100 miles (161 km) southeast of Pasadena, was a small town in those days and seemed to offer no threat to the dark night skies that optical astronomy demanded.

Meanwhile, the future telescope's giant mirror was being built. The Corning Glass Works in New York, chosen to make the mirror, decided to form it from Pyrex, a patented type of glass that resists changing shape in response to changes in temperature. (Even tiny shape changes can make a telescope mirror distort images or go out of focus.) In 1934, the company poured 21 tons (19 metric tons) of liquid Pyrex into a mold that gave the back of the mirror a partly hollow, honeycomb shape. This design made the mirror less than half as heavy as a solid piece of Pyrex of the same size would have been.

The great disc of glass had to be cooled very slowly over a period of 10 months so it would not warp or crack. It traveled from New York to Pasadena in its own special train in 1936. Workers at Caltech ground the front of the mirror to produce the necessary curved-in shape, then polished it, removing 10,000 pounds (4,540 kg) of glass in the process. Finally, they coated the glass with aluminum, which reflects light even better than silver does.

George Hale did not live to see the completion of his last dream. He died of heart disease in Pasadena on February 21, 1938, at age 69. World War II interrupted construction of the Mount Palomar observatory, so the observatory did not open until 1948. Its magnificent 200-inch telescope, then the largest single-mirror reflector in the world and still the second-largest, was dedicated on June 3 of that year. To the surprise of no one, the telescope was named for George Ellery Hale.

The largest optical telescopes today are built differently from those of Hale's time. Instead of having single mirrors, they use computers to combine views from several separate telescopes. This creates, in effect, a single telescope as large as all the individual ones put together. Although these modern telescopes are unlike the Hooker and Hale telescopes, they still owe their existence to George Hale's genius for "dreaming big" and persuading others to help him turn his dreams into reality. In a biographical article on Hale published in *Solar Physics* 30 years after his death, Harold Zirin of the Mount Wilson and Palomar Observatories wrote that "all Hale's major achievements, and those of his observatories, were made possible by the wide range of capability and vision he provided. . . . Hale's greatest monument is the achievement of astronomers all over the world who have profited from his works and built on them for deeper understanding of the universe."

Chronology

1815	Joseph von Fraunhofer invents spectroscope
1840	Henry Draper takes first astronomical photograph
1845	The third earl of Rosse builds large reflecting telescope nicknamed "the Leviathan"
1868	George Ellery Hale born in Chicago on June 29

1888	Lick Observatory completes world's largest refracting telescope, with a 36-inch (.91-m) lens
1889	Hale invents spectroheliograph
1890	In April, Hale uses spectroheliograph to photograph spectra of solar prominences in daylight for the first time; in June, he obtains bachelor's degree in physics from MIT and marries Evelina Conklin
1891	Kenwood Physical Observatory incorporated by state; Hale rejects offer to join University of Chicago
1892	Hale joins University of Chicago faculty as world's first professor of astrophysics on July 26; in late summer, he hears about two glass disks suitable to become lenses for a large refracting telescope; in October, he persuades Charles Tyson Yerkes to donate $1 million to University of Chicago to build a telescope and observatory
1894	Hale awarded Janssen Medal by French Academy of Sciences; he buys glass disk that could be made into a 60-inch (1.5-m) mirror for a reflecting telescope
1895	Hale shows that helium exists on Earth
1897	Yerkes Observatory's 40-inch (1.01-m) refracting telescope completed in May; floor under telescope collapses on May 28; after floor is repaired, observatory is dedicated on October 21
1890s	Hale begins to think of building a large reflecting telescope late in the decade
1902	On January 10, Hale sees article describing founding of Carnegie Institution and decides to ask the institution to fund his telescope project
1903	In June, Hale visits Mount Wilson for the first time; he moves to Pasadena with his family late in the year
1904	Hale wins Henry Draper Medal from the National Academy of Sciences; he signs 99-year lease for land on Mount Wilson;

	he learns on December 20 that Carnegie Institution will fund building of observatory on Mount Wilson
1905	On January 7, Hale resigns as director of Yerkes Observatory and becomes director of Mount Wilson Observatory; solar telescope and related facilities go into use at Mount Wilson; Hale makes first photographs of sunspot spectra; he concludes that sunspots are cooler than their surroundings
1908	Hale concludes that sunspots contain strong magnetic fields; 60-inch (1.5-m) reflecting telescope goes into use at Mount Wilson
1916	Hale wins Astronomical Society of the Pacific's Bruce Medal
1917	100-inch (2.5-m) Hooker Telescope goes into use at Mount Wilson
1922	Hale resigns as director of Mount Wilson
1920s	Late in the decade, Hale begins planning new observatory with a 200-inch (5.1-m) reflecting telescope
1928	Rockefeller Foundation offers $6.5 million to build observatory and telescope
1932	Hale wins Copley Medal from Britain's Royal Society
1934	Hale chooses Mount Palomar as site for new observatory; glass poured for 200-inch (5.1-m) telescope mirror
1936	Mirror travels by special train to Pasadena
1938	George Ellery Hale dies on February 21
1948	200-inch (5.1-m) telescope at Mount Palomar dedicated and named Hale Telescope on June 3

Further Reading

Books

Wright, Helen. *Explorer of the Universe: A Biography of George Ellery Hale.* New York: E. P. Dutton, 1966.
   Detailed, definitive biography of Hale.

Articles

Caltech Astronomy Department. "Palomar Observatory Timeline."
Available online. URL: http://www.astro.caltech.edu/observatories/
palomar/history. Accessed on September 26, 2005.
> Time line extending from 1908 to 1947 describes the construction of
> the Mount Palomar Observatory and 200-inch Hale telescope, with
> some information about the Mount Wilson Observatory as well.

Kelleher, Florence M. "George Ellery Hale (1868–1938)." Yerkes
Observatory Virtual Museum. Available online. URL: http://
astro.uchicago.edu/yerkes/virtualmuseum/Hale.html. Accessed on
September 26, 2005.
> Detailed biographical article on Hale focuses on his early years and his
> time at Yerkes Observatory.

Moreau, Dan. "Astrophysicist Named Sky-High Innovate." *Investor's
Business Daily,* February 19, 2003, A4.
> Brief, easy-to-read article summarizes Hale's career.

Sheehan, William, and Dan Koehler. "Yerkes at 100." *Astronomy* 25
(November 1997): 50–55.
> Article written on the centennial of the opening of the Yerkes
> Observatory describes the observatory's creation.

Zirin, Harold. "George Ellery Hale, 1868–1938." *Solar Physics* 5
(1968): 435–441.
> Interesting article on Hale's life and work, written on the 100th anni-
> versary of his birth.

2
GALAXIES GALORE

EDWIN HUBBLE AND THE EXPANDING UNIVERSE

Italian astronomer Galileo Galilei used a newly invented device called a telescope to turn the Renaissance world on its head 400 years ago. In the 1920s, another astronomer, Edwin Powell Hubble, changed human beings' picture of the universe almost as profoundly. Like Galileo, Hubble made his discoveries with the latest and best technology of his time—in Hubble's case, the 100-inch (2.5-m) Hooker telescope on Mount Wilson. George Ellery Hale, the man chiefly responsible for that telescope's existence, had personally invited Hubble to use it.

Humble Beginnings

George Hale was far from the only person whom Edwin Hubble impressed. Most people who knew Hubble apparently thought highly of him—including Hubble himself. In *Coming of Age in the Milky Way,* a book on the history of humankind's attempts to understand the universe, Timothy Ferris describes Hubble as "a tall, elegant, and overbearing man with a highly evolved opinion of his potential place in history."

Hubble may not have been modest, but he came from a modest background. He was born on November 20, 1889, in Marshfield, Missouri, to John and Virginia Hubble. John Hubble was an insurance agent. The Hubbles moved to Wheaton, Illinois, a suburb of Chicago, in 1898, and Edwin spent his teenage years there. He

Edwin Hubble showed that the universe consists of many galaxies, all racing away from one another as the universe expands. (Archives, California Institute of Technology, print 10.12-20)

was a star athlete in high school, excelling in football and track. His grades were also good enough to win him a place in the University of Chicago when he was only 16 years old.

Hubble studied mathematics, chemistry, physics, and astronomy at the university. He also made time for track, basketball, and boxing. He graduated with a bachelor's degree in physics in 1910, but his father and grandfather wanted him to be an attorney rather than a scientist. Supported by a prestigious Rhodes scholarship, he studied law at Queen's College, part of Britain's renowned Oxford University, between 1910 and 1913. Hubble's stay in England left him with a British accent and mannerisms that he kept for the rest of his life.

Mystery Clouds

Edwin Hubble's family had moved to Kentucky by the time he returned to the United States, so he went there as well. For a year or so, he taught Spanish and coached a basketball team at a high school in New Albany. He may also have practiced law in Louisville.

None of these activities involved astronomy, however, so Hubble was not happy with them. In spring 1914, he asked one of his former professors at the University of Chicago to help him return to the university as a graduate student. The professor obtained a scholarship for him at Yerkes Observatory, which George Ellery Hale had founded for the university in Williams Bay, Wisconsin.

At Yerkes, Hubble photographed mysterious objects called nebulae, a Latin word meaning "clouds." Nebulae were smudges of light in the night sky that did not move or change their appearance over time. Studies in the late 19th century had revealed that some nebulae were clouds of hot gas, but the nature of others, called spiral nebulae because of their shape as seen through large telescopes, was less clear.

Hubble's photos revealed 511 nebulae so faint that they had never been recognized in photographs before. He believed that their light was dim because they were very far away. Many lay outside the plane of the Milky Way galaxy, he pointed out. Like a few earlier astronomers, including William Herschel in the 18th century, Hubble speculated that some nebulae, including the ones he photographed, might be galaxies outside the Milky Way. In 1755, German philosopher Immanuel Kant had called these possible other systems "island universes." Most astronomers, however, including those of Hubble's own time, thought that the universe contained only the Milky Way galaxy.

From Battlefield to Mountaintop

In October 1916, George Ellery Hale offered Edwin Hubble a young astronomer's chance of a lifetime. Hale had met Hubble while Hubble was still an undergraduate at the University of Chicago and apparently had liked what he saw. Looking for the best astronomers to work with the Hooker Telescope, then almost completed, Hale asked Hubble to join the staff of the Mount Wilson Observatory as soon as Hubble had completed his doctorate.

Not surprisingly, Hubble accepted. Before he could take Hale up on his offer, however, the United States entered World War I. Deciding that patriotism was even more important than astronomy, Hubble enlisted in the army in May 1917, three days after he obtained his Ph.D. He took officer training and eventually was promoted to the rank of major. He went to France in September 1918, but the fighting ended before he saw battle.

Hubble was discharged from his military service on August 20, 1919. Still wearing his major's uniform, he headed for Mount Wilson as soon as he was back in the United States.

An Island Universe

Hubble continued his study of nebulae at Mount Wilson. On the night of October 5, 1923, he used the Hooker Telescope and its attached camera to make a long-exposure photograph of a large spiral nebula, known in astronomical catalogs as M31, in the constellation Andromeda. When he analyzed the photo, he saw what he was sure were individual stars within the nebula—something no one had observed before.

Several of the stars Hubble saw in M31 were very bright, and he thought at first that they were novas, or stars that suddenly become much brighter than usual because of an explosion in the gas surrounding them. On a hunch, however, he compared his photo with 60 others in the Mount Wilson archives, made of the same nebula at various times going back to 1909. The comparisons showed that one of his stars brightened, dimmed, and brightened again in a regular cycle. A nova would not act that way, Hubble knew, but such changes would be typical for another type of star, called a Cepheid variable.

Hubble was excited to find a possible Cepheid in M31 because astronomers about a decade earlier had developed a way to use Cepheids as "yardsticks" to determine the distance from Earth of the star formations in which the Cepheids were embedded. If the star in M31 really was a Cepheid, therefore, Hubble could use it to find out how far away the nebula was. Harlow Shapley, head of the Harvard Observatory, had recently calculated (also using Cepheids) that the Milky Way was 300,000 light-years across, so determining the distance to M31 would show whether or not the nebula was within the Milky Way. (A light-year is the distance that light, which moves at 186,000 miles [300,000 km] per second, can travel in a year—about 6 trillion miles [9.5 trillion km].)

Observing his star for a week in February 1924, Hubble confirmed that the star followed the pattern of brightness changes

This spiral galaxy in the constellation Andromeda, M31 in astronomical catalogs, was the first star system proven to exist outside the Milky Way. (Yerkes Observatory photograph G101)

expected for a Cepheid. Then, using this star as a distance marker, he calculated that M31 was about 930,000 light-years from Earth—more than three times Shapley's estimate for the width of the Milky Way. The nebula had to be another galaxy.

Hubble and Shapley did not like each other, either personally or professionally. (They had met at Mount Wilson in 1919, before Shapley moved to Harvard.) In contrast to Hubble, Shapley strongly believed that the Milky Way was the only galaxy in the universe. On February 19, 1924, according to Timothy Ferris, Hubble could not resist sending a deliberately understated note to his rival: "You will be interested to hear that I have found a Cepheid variable in the Andromeda Nebula."

Shapley's reply called Hubble's letter "the most entertaining piece of literature I have seen for some time." When the Harvard astronomer showed the letter to a friend, however, he said, "Here is the letter that has destroyed my universe."

Classifying Galaxies

Edwin Hubble's demonstration that the Milky Way was not the only galaxy in the cosmos shook the universes of many other astronomers besides Harlow Shapley. The astronomical community first heard about Hubble's discovery on New Year's Day 1925, in a paper presented at a joint meeting of the American Astronomical Society and the American Association for the Advancement of Science.

SOLVING PROBLEMS: STARRY YARDSTICKS

Before computing machines existed, the "computers" at the Harvard College Observatory were women. The observatory's director, Edward Pickering, hired them (at minimal salaries) to perform tedious tasks connected with astronomical photographs, such as counting stars in the photos and comparing the stars' brightness. Several of these women are now regarded as pioneer astronomers, and one of them, Henrietta Swan Leavitt, discovered the tool that let Edwin Hubble prove that the Andromeda nebula lay outside the Milky Way.

In 1907, Pickering assigned Leavitt to measure the brightness of stars in the observatory's photographs. She noticed that some stars dimmed and brightened on a regular schedule, and she began keeping a record of these "variable stars." She found some 2,400 of them, most never listed before, in two smudges called the Large and Small Magellanic Clouds (which, like M31, were later shown to be galaxies outside the Milky Way).

Many of the variable stars in the Small Magellanic Cloud belonged to a particular type called Cepheids. In 1912, Leavitt reported that the longer a Cepheid's period (the time of one cycle of brightening

Hubble also described his work in articles published in *Science* and several other journals later in 1925. The papers included analysis of multiple Cepheids that Hubble by then had identified in M31 and another spiral nebula, M33.

Hubble was now sure that the universe was studded with galaxies. Around 1926, he worked out a system of classifying these galaxies according to their shape. Many, like the Milky Way, were spirals, with arms curving out from a central disk. A small number of odd ones had two arms that extended straight out from a bulging center for a certain distance, then curled into a spiral shape. Hubble called these barred spirals. Still other galaxies lacked arms entirely and looked like flattened circles, or ellipses.

Hubble arranged his galaxy shapes in a two-pronged diagram that looked like a tuning fork or a sideways letter Y and showed

and dimming), the brighter the star appeared to be at its brightest. A star's apparent brightness is affected by its distance from Earth, but all the Cepheids in the cloud were considered to be about equally far away. Leavitt concluded, therefore, that the relationship she had noted must apply to the stars' true, or absolute, brightness. It was as though all lighthouse beacons with 100,000-watt light bulbs rotated once a minute, and all those with 200,000-watt bulbs rotated once every two minutes.

Leavitt would have liked to follow up on her observation, but Pickering kept her busy measuring stars instead. Other astronomers, however, realized that her discovery meant that if a Cepheid's period was known, its absolute brightness could be calculated. Once its true brightness was determined, that figure could be compared with its apparent brightness, and the comparison, in turn, would yield the star's distance from Earth. (The farther away a light is from an observer, the dimmer the light will appear to be. The headlights of a car seen from a mile away will look four times dimmer than those of an identical car seen from half a mile away.) By using Cepheids as yardsticks, astronomers could find the distance of any group of stars in which Cepheids were embedded. This had become a standard method of calculating astronomical distances by Edwin Hubble's time.

what he believed were two possible paths that galaxies might follow as they evolved, or changed with age. Astronomers still use his classification system, although they no longer believe that it reflects the evolution of galaxies.

Shifting Spectra

Hubble began investigating a different aspect of galaxies in the late 1920s, using the spectroscope attached to the Hooker Telescope. Astronomers had learned that a phenomenon called the Doppler shift, which Austrian physicist Christian Doppler had discovered

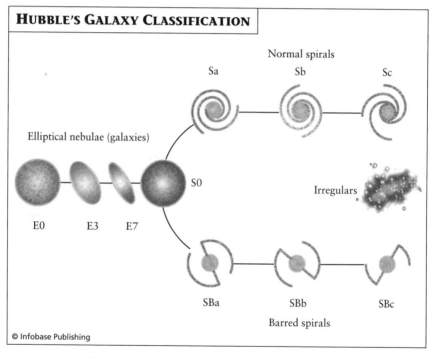

HUBBLE'S GALAXY CLASSIFICATION

Normal spirals

Sa   Sb   Sc

Elliptical nebulae (galaxies)

S0

Irregulars

E0   E3   E7

SBa   SBb   SBc

Barred spirals

© Infobase Publishing

Astronomers still use Edwin Hubble's classification of galaxies according to their shape, although they no longer share Hubble's belief that this classification system shows how galaxies evolve.

in 1842, let them use the spectra of stars and other astronomical objects to determine the direction and speed of the objects' motion. Hubble applied the Doppler shift to galaxies.

Doppler had noticed that a sound, such as a train whistle, appears to rise in pitch when the source of the sound moves toward to an observer. Conversely, when the sound source moves away from the observer, the pitch of the sound drops. The faster the object is moving, the more the pitch changes.

Light, like sound, is a form of radiation, and British astronomer William Huggins speculated in 1866 that spectra from astronomical sources would also show Doppler shifts. If a star, for instance, was moving toward Earth, all the lines in the spectrum made from that star's light would be pushed closer to the violet end of the spectral range than they would have been if the star were standing still relative to the Earth. The further toward the violet the lines were shifted, the faster the star would be moving. Similarly, if the light source was moving away from Earth, all its spectral lines would be shifted toward the red end of the spectrum. Huggins's idea proved to be correct, and by Hubble's time, astronomers regularly used Doppler shifts to measure the velocities of stars within the Milky Way galaxy.

Vesto M. Slipher, an astronomer at the Lowell Observatory in Flagstaff, Arizona, had detected Doppler shifts in the spectra of spiral nebulae as early as 1912. The blue shift he found in the spectrum from M31, the same nebula that Hubble later showed to be a separate galaxy, suggested that the nebula was rushing toward Earth at 180 miles (300 km) per second. By 1917, Slipher had analyzed 24 more spiral nebulae and found that, unlike M31, they appeared to be moving away from Earth: Their spectra were all shifted toward the red.

In the late 1920s, Hubble asked Milton L. Humason, another Mount Wilson staff member, to make spectra of certain galaxies and calculate the galaxies' speed from their redshifts. Humason also worked out the speeds of some of the galaxies that Slipher had analyzed. Hubble himself used Cepheid "yardsticks" to determine how far from Earth those same galaxies were.

After studying about two dozen galaxies, Hubble concluded in 1929 that almost every galaxy he could measure was receding from

Earth, just as Slipher had reported. Furthermore, the farther away the galaxies were, the faster they seemed to be moving. Some had redshifts that suggested velocities of more than 600 miles (1,000 km) per second. This direct proportional relationship between speed and distance came to be called Hubble's Law.

Donald E. Osterbrock and his coauthors wrote that the paper in which Hubble announced his discovery, "A Relation between Distance and Radial Velocity among Extra-Galactic Nebulae," "sent shock waves through the astronomical community." At the same time, according to Allan Sandage, the paper "was written so convincingly that it was believed almost immediately."

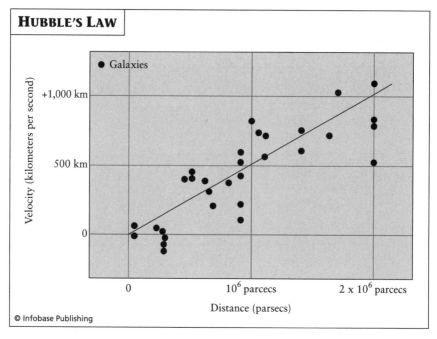

Edwin Hubble compared the distance of galaxies (measured in parsecs; a parsec is about 3.25 light-years) with the speed of their motion away from Earth and found that these two quantities bore a simple relationship to each other: The farther from Earth a galaxy is, the faster it is moving. (The straight line on the diagram shows the relationship, averaged from the figures for individual galaxies.) This relationship, called Hubble's Law, proved that the universe is expanding.

Runaway Universe

For some reason, Allan Sandage writes, Edwin Hubble "was remarkably silent about the meaning of what he and Humason had found. . . . Neither in his personal conversations nor in his writings did he discuss its implications for ideas about either the evolution of the universe from a primitive state or its meaning concerning a 'creation event.' " Indeed, Hubble claimed all his life that some effect other than movement might produce an "apparent" redshift in the spectra of distant galaxies.

Other astronomers, however, grasped the implications of Hubble's discovery at once. If redshifts really did reflect galaxies' movement, the universe had to be expanding, like a balloon slowly filling with air. As space itself stretched, all the galaxies in it were pushed farther and farther away from each other. In turn, the idea that the universe was expanding suggested that the expansion must have started from some central point at some time in the past.

Among the scientists most eager to accept Hubble's research was Albert Einstein, whose general theory of relativity had predicted in 1915 that the universe would prove to be either expanding or contracting. Astronomers had insisted so strongly that the universe must be unchanging, however, that in 1917 Einstein inserted a "cosmological constant" into his formulas to make them fit this belief. After seeing Hubble's work, Einstein concluded that his theory had been right the first time and restored his original equations. On a visit to Mount Wilson in 1931, Einstein personally thanked Hubble for having freed him from the cosmological constant, which the great physicist called the greatest mistake of his life.

Astronomy Star

Hubble continued his work in the 1930s, confirming his redshift findings and extending them to galaxies farther and farther away from Earth. Wanting to study galaxies even fainter than those that the Hooker Telescope could reveal, he helped George Ellery Hale set up Hale's new observatory on Mount Palomar and greatly looked forward to being able to use the 200-inch (5.1-m) telescope being built there.

By the end of the decade, Hubble was famous. He had won virtually every award in astronomy, including the Bruce Medal of the Astronomical Society of the Pacific (1938), the Benjamin Franklin Medal of the Franklin Institute (1939), and the Gold Medal of the Royal Astronomical Society (1940). His fame, furthermore, extended well beyond the astronomical community. For instance, one of several popular books he wrote about astronomy, *The Realm of the Nebulae*, became a best seller when it was published in 1936.

With his well-tailored clothes, British accent, and pipe, Edwin Hubble was the perfect picture of a distinguished scientist, and people were eager to meet him. He and his wife, Grace, whom he had married in 1924, attended many Hollywood parties in the 1930s and 1940s and became friends with film personalities such as Charlie Chaplin. Donald Osterbrock and his coauthors wrote that Hubble's "compelling personality seemed less like those of other astronomers than like those of the movie stars and writers who became his friends in the later years of his life."

Hubble took a break from his astronomical work during World War II, just as he had in World War I. This time he worked at the U.S. Army's Ballistics Research Laboratory at the Aberdeen Proving Ground in Maryland, calculating the flight paths of artillery shells. After the war, when the 200-inch (5.1-m) Hale Telescope finally went into operation on Mount Palomar in 1948, Hubble was the first astronomer allowed to use it. Sadly, he was not able to work with it for long. Hubble died of a stroke at age 63 in San Marino, California, on September 28, 1953.

Just as George Ellery Hale had left a legacy of new telescopes with unimaginable power, Edwin Hubble left a heritage of puzzles for people using those telescopes to explore. With his demonstration of the expanding universe, Hubble founded a new field of astronomy: observational cosmology. Before his time, cosmology—the study of the origin, evolution, and structure of the universe—had been more the province of theologians and philosophers than of scientists. Hubble, however, showed that conclusions about these matters could be drawn from and tested by observable physical facts. As Donald Osterbrock and his coauthors wrote in *Scientific American,* "Hubble's energetic drive, keen intellect and supple communication skills enabled him to seize the problem of the construction of the universe and make it peculiarly his own."

Chronology

| 1889 | Edwin Hubble born in Marshfield, Missouri, on November 20 |
| 1898 | Hubble family moves to Wheaton, Illinois |

1910	Hubble earns B.S. in physics from University of Chicago
1912	Henrietta Leavitt discovers that Cepheid variable stars can be used to determine distances of faraway astronomical objects
1910–13	Hubble studies law at Queen's College (Oxford University), England, on Rhodes scholarship
1914–17	Hubble photographs faint nebulae at Yerkes Observatory
1915	Albert Einstein's general theory of relativity predicts that the universe will either expand or contract over time
1916	In October, George Ellery Hale offers Hubble a staff position at Mount Wilson Observatory
1917	Vesto Slipher publishes analysis of Doppler shifts in spectra of 25 spiral nebulae, showing that most of the nebulae are moving away from Earth; Einstein adds cosmological constant to his relativity equations to make them show an unchanging universe; Hubble earns Ph.D. from University of Chicago and enlists in U.S. Army
1919	Hubble is discharged from the army, returns to United States, and joins staff of Mount Wilson Observatory in August
1923	On October 5, Hubble makes photograph of Andromeda nebula (M31) containing what appears to be a Cepheid variable
1924	In February, Hubble confirms identification of Cepheid in M31 and uses the star to determine the nebula's distance from Earth
1925	On January 1, scientific meeting hears Hubble's paper proving that M31 and another spiral nebula lie outside the Milky Way and are probably independent galaxies
1926	Hubble devises classification system for galaxies
1929	On March 15, Hubble publishes paper showing that most galaxies are moving away from Earth and that the farther away they are, the faster they are moving

1930s	Hubble extends redshift research to fainter and fainter galaxies, helps George Ellery Hale set up Mount Palomar Observatory, and becomes friends with movie stars and famous people
1931	Einstein thanks Hubble for restoring his faith in the original version of his general theory of relativity
1936	Hubble publishes *Realm of the Nebulae*
1938	Hubble wins Bruce Medal
1939	Hubble wins Benjamin Franklin Medal
1940	Hubble wins Gold Medal of Royal Astronomical Society
1940–45	Hubble calculates flight paths of artillery shells at Aberdeen Proving Ground
1948	Hubble becomes first astronomer to use Mount Palomar's Hale Telescope
1953	Hubble dies of a stroke in San Marino, California, on September 28

Further Reading

Books

Bartusiak, Marcia, ed. *Archives of the Universe: A Treasury of Astronomy's Historic Works of Discovery.* New York: Pantheon Books, 2004.

Includes reprints of Hubble's two most important papers, "Cepheids in Spiral Nebulae" and "A Relation between Distance and Radial Velocity among Extra-Galactic Nebulae," with commentary.

Christianson, Gale E. *Edwin Hubble: Mariner of the Nebulae.* New York: Farrar, Straus and Giroux, 1995.

Full-length, detailed biography of Hubble.

Ferris, Timothy. *Coming of Age in the Milky Way.* New York: William Morrow, 1988.

History of humans' attempts to understand their place in the physical universe tells how Edwin Hubble's discoveries changed astronomers' picture of the cosmos.

Hubble, Edwin. *The Realm of the Nebulae.* Oxford: Oxford University Press, 1936.
> Reprint of the Silliman Lectures, given at Yale University, in which Hubble describes his research for nonscientists.

Sharov, Alexander S., and Igor D. Novikov. *Edwin Hubble, the Discoverer of the Big Bang Universe.* Cambridge: Cambridge University Press, 1993.
> Short translated book by two Russian astronomers is divided into a section on Hubble's life and work and a section on later discoveries based on Hubble's findings.

Articles

"Admiral of the Starry Sea." *U.S. News & World Report* 125 (August 17, 1998), 48–52.
> Popular magazine article describing Edwin Hubble's personality and achievements.

Christianson, Gale. "Mastering the Universe." *Astronomy* 27 (February 1999): 60ff.
> Hubble's chief biographer portrays highlights of his life and work.

Lemonick, Michael D. "The Astronomer." *Time* 153 (March 29, 1999), 124ff.
> Popular article about Hubble's career and discoveries.

Osterbrock, Donald E., Joel A. Gwinn, and Ronald S. Brashear. "Edwin Hubble and the Expanding Universe." *Scientific American* 269 (July 1993), 84–89.
> Detailed biographical article about Hubble and his discoveries.

Sandage, Allan. "Edwin Hubble 1889–1953." *Journal of the Royal Astronomical Society of Canada* 83 (December 1989).
> Article written on the centennial of Hubble's birth that concentrates on Hubble's work, especially his four most important achievements.

Web Site

EdwinHubble.com. URL: http://www.edwinhubble.com. Accessed on January 29, 2005.
> Site devoted to Hubble includes a brief biography, quotes, images, an interactive "stargazer" diagram, references, and links.

3
BIG EARS

GROTE REBER AND RADIO ASTRONOMY

A folk story from India tells about six blind men who encountered an elephant for the first time. Each touched a different part of the gigantic animal and assumed that the whole creature was just like the part he felt. They therefore came to completely different conclusions about what an elephant was. One man stroked the elephant's trunk, for instance, and decided that an elephant was like a snake. Another bumped into the elephant's side and said the beast resembled a wall. The man who touched the elephant's ear was equally sure that elephants were immense fans.

Until the mid-20th century, astronomers were much like these confused men. The huge telescopes that Hale and others built could detect only 200ths of 1 percent of the range of radiation that reaches Earth from space. As a result, astronomers' picture of the universe was far from complete.

Grote Reber built the first radio telescope in his backyard in 1937, a year after this photograph was taken. (National Radio Astronomy Observatory/AUI/NSF)

35

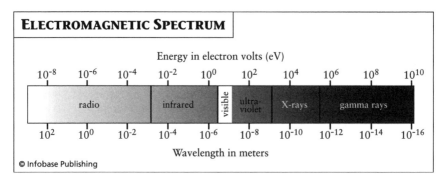

Light makes up just a small part of the full range, or spectrum, of electromagnetic radiation.

Invisible Light

Scientists had known since the 19th century that forms of radiation invisible to the human eye existed. In the 1860s and 1870s, British mathematician and physicist James Clerk Maxwell predicted that light would prove to be just one form of what came to be called electromagnetic radiation. Heinrich Hertz, a German physicist, proved in 1888 that Maxwell's electromagnetic waves were real. In that same year, Hertz produced radio waves in his laboratory for the first time.

Radiation can be pictured either as waves of different lengths or as streams of particles. The whole spectrum of visible light, from red (which has the longest wavelength) to violet (which has the shortest), makes up only 2 percent of the electromagnetic spectrum, the full range of electromagnetic radiation. Types of electromagnetic waves shorter than those of visible light include ultraviolet light, X-rays, and radiation with very high energy called gamma rays. Waves longer than visible light include infrared waves, microwaves, and radio waves.

As soon as scientists realized the extent of the electromagnetic spectrum, some began to wonder whether objects in the heavens might give off forms of radiation besides light. Experimenters tried to detect radio waves from the Sun in the 1890s, but their radio receivers were too insensitive to pick up the Sun's weak signals. Most astronomers concluded that radio signals from outside the Earth, if they did exist, could not be detected.

Jansky's Merry-Go-Round

Radio waves proved very useful in long-distance communication, however. Guglielmo Marconi, an Italian-born inventor, developed the first practical radio communication system in 1901. Companies began using radio to extend telephone service across the Atlantic Ocean around 1925. In 1928, wanting to expand and improve this service, Bell Telephone Laboratories assigned Karl Jansky, a young man who had just started working for the company, to find out what sources of interference (noise, or static) might block transmission of short radio waves.

Jansky had to invent most of the equipment he used for this task. He built a rickety-looking, 100-foot (30-m)-long antenna in a field near the Bell laboratory in Holmdel, New Jersey, in 1930. The antenna could be moved around a circular track, allowing Jansky to measure signals coming from different directions. Jansky called it his merry-go-round.

Throughout 1931, Jansky recorded interference from different parts of the sky at different times of day. He presented his analysis of the results in "Directional Studies of Atmospherics at High Frequencies," a paper delivered to

Bell Telephone Laboratories engineer Karl Jansky built this movable radio antenna in a field near Holmdel, New Jersey, in 1930 and called it his "merry-go-round." With it, he detected a mysterious radio hiss that proved to come from outside the solar system. (National Radio Astronomy Observatory/AUI/NSF)

the International Scientific Radio Union in April 1932. In this paper, he described three types of interference: static caused by lightning in nearby thunderstorms, static arising from more distant storms, and a "third group [of sounds] . . . composed of very steady hiss static the origin of which is not yet known."

OTHER SCIENTISTS: KARL JANSKY

The skills in physics and engineering that had brought Karl Guthe Jansky to Bell Laboratories came naturally. Born on October 22, 1905, in Norman, Oklahoma, Jansky was the third son of Cyril M. Jansky, then dean of the College of Engineering at the University of Oklahoma, Norman. Karl Jansky's oldest brother, C. M. Jansky, Jr., also became a radio engineer.

The Jansky family moved to Madison, Wisconsin, when Karl was three years old. Cyril Jansky joined the faculty of the University of Wisconsin in that city, and Karl earned a bachelor of science degree in physics, with honors, from the same university in 1927. (He obtained a master's degree in 1936.) Soon after his graduation, Karl Jansky applied to Bell Laboratories for a job, but the company was reluctant to hire the young man at first because Jansky suffered from lifelong kidney disease. Fortunately, Karl's engineer brother knew people in the laboratory's personnel department and persuaded them that Karl would be a dependable employee.

After he detected radio waves that he believed were coming from the Milky Way, Karl Jansky began studying astronomy in his spare time in the hope of following up his observations. His employers at Bell Laboratories, however, concluded that Jansky's hiss was too weak to interfere with transatlantic shortwave radio transmission, and that was all they wanted to know about it. They assigned Jansky to other tasks, and he was never able to return to his astronomy studies.

Jansky died on February 14, 1950, in Red Bank, New Jersey, at the young age of 44, of a stroke probably brought on by his kidney disease. During his lifetime, he received no honors for his discovery of extraterrestrial radio emissions, but in 1973, the unit used to measure the strength, or flux density, of a radio source was named after him. This unit, the jansky, is abbreviated Jy.

Jansky continued to study his mystery hiss during 1932 and found that it completed a cycle of rising and falling intensity once a day. At first he thought that the interfering radio waves might come from the Sun. After a few months, however, he saw that the direction of the most intense waves no longer matched that of the Sun. Careful analysis showed, furthermore, that the waves' intensity cycle took 23 hours and 56 minutes, not 24 hours, which meant that the radio cycle matched the timing of the Earth's rotation in relation to the stars rather than its rotation relative to the Sun. This fact suggested that the static came from outside the solar system.

Tracing the most intense radio signals to a spot in the constellation Sagittarius that corresponded to the center of the Earth's home galaxy, the Milky Way, Jansky concluded that the galactic center was the most likely source of the radio waves. He suspected that ionized, or electrically charged, gas between the stars gave off the radio static. He presented a paper describing his conclusions, cautiously titled "Electrical Disturbances Apparently of Extraterrestrial Origin," at a meeting of the International Scientific Radio Union in April 1933.

The First Radio Telescope

Professional astronomers showed no interest in Karl Jansky's puzzling hiss, but one amateur astronomer felt differently. Grote Reber, born in Chicago on December 22, 1911, heard about Jansky's work in 1933 and concluded that the Bell engineer had made, as an article by Dave Finley in *Mercury* quotes Reber as saying, "a fundamental and very important discovery."

Reber, who had just graduated from the Illinois Institute of Technology with a B.S. in engineering, asked Bell Laboratories for a job in the hope of working with Jansky. Jobs were scarce during the Great Depression, however, and Bell did not hire him. Instead, Reber went to work designing radio receivers for a manufacturer in Chicago. He vowed to follow up Jansky's research in his spare time.

In 1937, with the help of friends, Reber built a giant radio receiving antenna—essentially the first radio telescope—in his backyard in Wheaton, the same suburb of Chicago where Edwin Hubble had spent his teen years. It cost about a third of his salary for the year. Reber's telescope weighed two tons (1.8 metric tons) and had a galvanized iron mirror 31.4 feet (9 m) in diameter. Like the mirrors of George Ellery Hale's giant reflecting telescopes and the much smaller satellite television dishes that some homes have today, Reber's mirror had the shape of a parabola. A parabolic mirror focuses all waves on the same point, regardless of their wavelength.

Radio waves striking Reber's dish, which could be turned to point at different parts of the sky, were reflected and focused on a metal cylinder suspended 20 feet (6 m) above the mirror. The cylinder contained a radio receiver, which amplified the faint signals millions of times to make them strong enough to be detected. The receiver then translated the radio waves into electric signals that could be recorded as ink tracings on paper.

Maps of the Radio Sky

Reber began using his telescope in 1938. He collected most of his data in the hours before dawn because static from the sparks in automobile engines drowned out the weak interstellar signals during the day. He had to try three receivers, tuned to different wavelengths, before he found one that worked. Finally, late in the year, Reber detected the same kind of radiation from the Milky Way that Jansky had found.

In the early 1940s, Reber translated systematic observations with his dish into the first radio maps of the sky. He drew them as contour maps, much like those that geologists and surveyors use to show shapes and elevations of land. Reber's maps, however, showed radio "brightness," or intensity, instead of height.

Like Jansky, Reber found the strongest signals coming from the direction of the center of the Milky Way. Reber also detected bright radio sources in the constellations of Cygnus and Cassiopeia. He published his maps in various engineering and astronomy journals, beginning in 1941 and ending with a complete sky map in 1944.

Reber's work attracted little attention at first. For one thing, his maps appeared during World War II, when scientists and everyone else had more important things on their minds.

Furthermore, the two groups to whom Reber's findings might matter—radio engineers and astronomers—had no understanding of each other's fields. In fact, the first article about radio astronomy to appear in an astronomical journal, a paper Reber wrote about "cosmic static" that was published in the June 1940 *Astrophysical Journal,* was nearly rejected because the editor was unable to find any scientist with the right knowledge to review the article's accuracy.

A Farsighted Prediction

Fortunately, a few astronomers were more imaginative than the rest. Although Germany's Nazi government had taken over the Netherlands and partly cut that country off from the world, Jan Oort, director of the Leiden Observatory, happened to see Reber's 1940 *Astrophysical Journal* article and was greatly intrigued by it. Oort had been frustrated by the dark clouds of interstellar dust that obscured the center of the Milky Way galaxy, completely absorbing the light of stars more than a few thousand light-years away. He thought that radio waves might penetrate these clouds, allowing images of the galactic center to be created.

Oort also realized that if a large number of astronomical objects proved to give off radio waves of a specific wavelength, creating a fixed line on the electromagnetic spectrum, the position of that line would be shifted by the Doppler effect, just as spectral lines made by visible starlight were. Studying this shift would let astronomers measure the distance and movement of objects that did not give off light, such as the gas clouds themselves. Oort thought that radio waves might also offer a way to determine how fast the Milky Way was spinning around its center and how matter was distributed within it.

Oort told one of his students, Hendrik Van de Hulst, to look for radio wavelengths that might be used in this way. In 1945, Van de Hulst predicted that atoms of hydrogen, the most common element in the universe, would give off radio waves 21 centimeters (about 8 in.) long. He recommended that astronomers build antennae to look for this signal.

Early Achievements

Van de Hulst's prediction appeared just as World War II was ending. After the war, physicists and engineers who had gained experience with radio and electronics during the fighting were eager to use their new knowledge and equipment for peaceful purposes. Unlike most traditional astronomers, they saw exciting possibilities in radio astronomy. Some helped to set up radio astronomy observatories, such as the Jodrell Bank Observatory at the University of Manchester in England.

One of radio astronomy's first accomplishments was confirming Van de Hulst's prediction. Harold Ewen and Edward Purcell of Harvard University's Lyman Laboratory recorded 21-centimeter (about 8-in.) hydrogen radiation from the Milky Way for the first time on March 25, 1951, using a horn antenna that they had built from plywood and copper and attached to a fourth-floor window of the laboratory. (By international convention, radio wavelengths are always given in centimeters.) The antenna was a sloping structure with a large rectangular opening that tilted upward. This shape and angle, unfortunately, made the opening a perfect funnel for rainwater, often flooding the lab during storms, and a tempting target for snowballs thrown by passing students.

As Oort had suggested, radio astronomers used the hydrogen emission to determine the shape of the Milky Way galaxy, which proved to be a spiral like Andromeda and many other known galaxies. They also applied this new tool to mapping the large-scale distribution of matter in the galaxy. More and more astronomers began to realize that radio astronomy could answer many puzzles that optical astronomy had never solved.

A Long-Lived Pioneer

Grote Reber, meanwhile, continued to help radio astronomy develop. He left his manufacturing job in 1947 to work as a radio physicist at the National Bureau of Standards in Washington, D.C., where he remained until 1951. By this time, Reber was most interested in studying radio signals with long wavelengths. He helped to set up a radio telescope on the Hawaiian island of Maui to receive such waves in 1951.

In 1954, Reber moved to Tasmania, a large island off southeastern Australia. Tasmania is one of the few places in the world where long radio waves can penetrate the Earth's atmosphere, and it is almost the only place from which an astronomer can receive these waves from the center of the Milky Way. In his new home, Reber designed

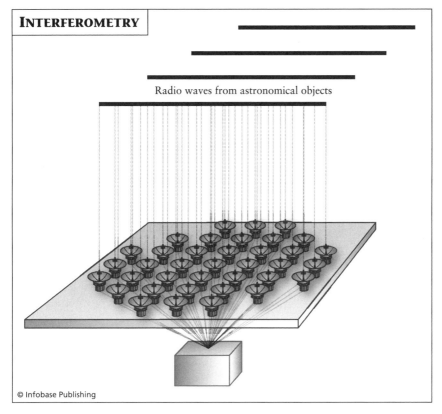

INTERFEROMETRY

Radio waves from astronomical objects

© Infobase Publishing

Interferometry combines data from many radio telescopes to create a "virtual dish" as large as the distances of all the telescopes put together. Cables, microwave links, or optical fibers connect the telescopes to a computer that combines all the telescopes' data into a single signal. The interferometer can also adjust the telescopes' signals to focus on particular objects in the sky.

and built a circular group of antennae with a diameter of 3,520 feet (1,073 m). He continued his research in Tasmania until his death on December 20, 2002, just two days short of his 91st birthday.

Unlike Karl Jansky, Reber lived long enough to be honored for his work. He won the Astronomical Society of the Pacific's

---

SOLVING PROBLEMS: INTERFEROMETRY AND "VIRTUAL DISHES"

To increase the size and accuracy of radio telescopes, astronomers have moved beyond single dishes. Because radio signals can be sent over large distances without distortion, radio astronomers can combine multiple telescopes at different locations to create a single, immense "virtual dish." The individual telescopes record radio waves from the same object at exactly the same time. The recordings are combined to create what is termed an *interference pattern*. Computers interpret the pattern to produce an image of the radio source.

Some radio astronomy observatories have many dishes working together in a single installation. The best-known observatory of this kind is the Very Large Array (VLA), located in an ancient lake bed near Socorro, New Mexico. The VLA, managed by the National Radio Astronomy Observatory, contains 27 steerable dish antennae, each 85 feet (26 m) wide, arranged in a Y-shaped pattern. Because the dishes are relatively close together, information from them can be sent to a single receiving set and merged as it is recorded.

Other radio astronomy observatories use a technique called very long baseline interferometry to combine information from telescopes in widely separated parts of the Earth. The telescopes are too far apart to allow their data to be blended in real time. Each telescope's data, therefore, are recorded on videotape at the site, and atomic clocks time the recording with great precision. When observation is completed, astronomers take the tapes from all the sites to a central location, synchronize them within a few millionths of a second, and play them together to produce a single signal that computers can analyze. The accuracy obtained in this way is as great as for a telescope with an antenna as wide as the distance between the actual telescopes.

Bruce Medal and the American Astronomical Society's Henry Norris Russell Lectureship in 1962, the Elliot Cresson medal of the Franklin Institute (Philadelphia) in 1963, the Jansky Prize of the National Radio Astronomy Observatory in 1975, and the Jackson-Gwilt Medal, the highest honor awarded by Britain's Royal Astronomical Society, in 1983. Ohio State University, Columbus, one of the first U.S. universities to sponsor radio astronomy research, awarded him an honorary doctorate of science in 1962, hailing him as "the foremost pioneer in this new field."

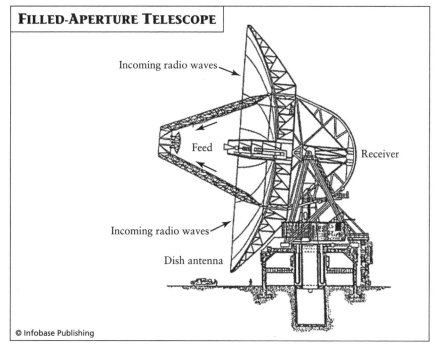

In a filled-aperture telescope, the most common kind of radio telescope, radio waves from space strike a large, curved ("dish") mirror antenna. The waves are reflected from the large mirror and focused on a smaller antenna above the mirror, called a feed. The feed, in turn, sends the waves down a cable to a receiver, usually located behind the main mirror. The receiver amplifies, or strengthens, and records the radio signals.

Radio Telescopes Today

Although radio telescopes have sometimes been called "big ears," they do not translate radio waves into sound as Karl Jansky's did. Instead, the telescopes' receivers record signals directly and send them to be processed and analyzed by computer. With suitable software, computers can translate radio data into visible images. Earth-based radio telescopes can receive waves between one and 21 centimeters (.4 and 8 in.) long, with little distortion by the atmosphere. However, the ionosphere, the atmosphere's charged upper layer, distorts or blocks longer wavelengths.

The most common kind of modern radio telescope, the filled-aperture telescope, is not too different from Grote Reber's backyard dish. This type of telescope has a large, parabolic antenna that gathers radio waves and a receiver that amplifies and records them. Unlike the case with Reber's dish, modern filled-aperture telescope receivers are usually located below and behind the dish rather than above it. The dish antenna focuses radio waves on a small second antenna above the dish, called a feed, and the feed sends the waves back down a cable to the receiver. Some telescopes have multiple feeds and receivers.

The resolution, or power to capture fine detail, of a radio telescope depends on the length of the waves divided by the size of the antenna. As with optical telescope mirrors, the larger a radio telescope antenna is, the more radiation it can gather and the more sensitive to weak signals it will be. Because radio waves from cosmic sources are very long, compared to other electromagnetic waves, and also very weak, the antennae used in radio astronomy must be far larger than the mirrors of even the hugest optical telescopes. The largest single radio telescope in the world, a nonsteerable dish, is in a bowl-shaped valley in Arecibo, Puerto Rico. Covered in 39,000 sheets of aluminum, it is 1,000 feet (305 m) across, 167 feet (51 m) deep, and covers about 20 acres (8.1 sq. hm).

Using radio telescopes, astronomers have discovered objects that probably could have been found in no other way. These include pulsars—small, rapidly spinning, extremely dense stars created by gigantic explosions—and quasars (short for *quasi-stellar radio sources*), starlike sources of powerful radio waves that are probably distant galaxies. Radio astronomy has revealed a violent cosmos, full of colliding galaxies and exploding stars. Dave Finley quotes Fred Lo, director of the National Radio Astronomy Observatory, as saying in 2002, "Radio astronomy has changed profoundly our understanding of the universe."

Chronology

1860s–70s	James Clerk Maxwell shows that electricity and magnetism are aspects of the same force and predicts that light will prove to be only a small part of a spectrum of electromagnetic radiation
1888	Heinrich Hertz proves that electromagnetic radiation exists and generates radio waves in his laboratory
1890s	Scientists attempt unsuccessfully to detect radio waves from the Sun
1901	Guglielmo Marconi develops first practical long-distance radio communication system
1905	Karl Guthe Jansky born in Norman, Oklahoma, on October 22
1911	Grote Reber born in Chicago on December 22
1925	Radiotelephone service across the Atlantic Ocean is established
1927	Karl Jansky earns B.S. in physics from University of Wisconsin, Madison
1928	Jansky begins working for Bell Telephone Laboratories and is assigned to find out what types of interference might block short radio waves
1929–30	Jansky builds "merry-go-round" antenna in Holmdel, New Jersey
1931	Jansky records radio interference (static) from different parts of the sky

1932	In April, Jansky presents paper describing three types and sources of static, including a hiss of unknown origin
1933	In April, Jansky presents paper concluding that the previously unknown static probably comes from the center of the Milky Way galaxy; Grote Reber obtains B.S. in engineering from Illinois Institute of Technology
1937	Reber builds radio telescope in his backyard
1938	Reber confirms Jansky's observation of radio emission from the Milky Way
1940	In June, an article about radio astronomy is published in an astronomy journal for the first time
1941–44	Reber makes maps of the sky showing sources of radio wave emission
1945	Hendrik Van de Hulst predicts that interstellar hydrogen will give off 21-centimeter (about 8-in.) radio waves; World War II ends
1947	Reber becomes radio physicist at National Bureau of Standards
1950	Jansky dies on February 14
1951	On March 25, Harold Ewen and Edward Purcell detect 21-centimeter (about 8-in.) hydrogen radiation from the Milky Way; Reber leaves National Bureau of Standards and helps to set up radio telescope in Maui, Hawaii
1954	Reber moves to Tasmania to study extraterrestrial radio signals with long wavelengths
1962	Reber receives Bruce Medal and Henry Norris Russell Lectureship
1983	Reber receives Jackson-Gwilt Medal from Royal Astronomical Society
2002	Reber dies on December 20 in Tasmania

Further Reading

Books

Voyage through the Universe: The New Astronomy. Alexandria, Va.: Time-Life Books, 1989.
> Includes material on the development of radio astronomy and how modern radio telescopes work.

Sullivan, W. T., ed. *The Early Years of Radio Astronomy.* New York: Cambridge University Press, 1984.
> Contains recollections of the pioneers of radio astronomy, covering the first 50 years of the science's development.

Articles

Finley, Dave. "Grote Reber (1911–2002)." *Mercury* 32 (March–April 2003): 6.
> Brief obituary listing Reber's achievements.

———. "Radio Astronomy Pioneer Grote Reber, ex-W9GFZ, SK." ARRL [American Radio Relay League] Web. December 23, 2002. Available online. URL: http://www.arrl.org/news/stories/2002/12/23/2/?nc=1. Accessed on February 2, 2005.
> Obituary describing Reber's founding of radio astronomy.

Ghigo, F. "Grote Reber and His Radio Telescope." National Radio Astronomy Observatory. Available online. URL: http://www.nrao.edu/whatisra/hist_reber.shtml. Accessed on January 29, 2005.
> Describes how Grote Reber, building on Karl Jansky's discovery of extraterrestrial radio signals, created the first radio maps of the sky in the early 1940s.

———. "Pre-History of Radio Astronomy." National Radio Astronomy Observatory. Available online. URL: http://www.nrao.edu/whatisra/hist_prehist.shtml. Accessed on January 29, 2005.
> Brief accounts of discoveries by James Clerk Maxwell and others that laid the groundwork for the development of radio astronomy.

Jansky, C. M., Jr. "My Brother Karl Jansky and His Discovery of Radio Waves from beyond the Earth." *Cosmic Search* 1, no. 4. Available online. URL: http://www.bigear.org/vol1no4/jansky.htm. Accessed on January 29, 2005.
> Reminiscences by Karl Jansky's older brother, given in a speech to the American Astronomical Society in 1956.

Jansky, Karl. "Directional Studies of Atmospherics at High Frequencies." *Proceedings of the Institute of Radio Engineers* 20 (1932).

> Article in which Karl Jansky described three kinds of static interfering with short-wave radio, including a steady hiss that he could not then identify.

———. "Electrical Disturbances Apparently of Extraterrestrial Origin." *Proceedings of the Institute of Radio Engineers* 21 (1933).

> Article in which Karl Jansky concluded that the mystery static was probably coming from the center of the Milky Way galaxy.

Kraus, John D. "Grote Reber, Founder of Radio Astronomy." *Journal of the Royal Astronomical Society of Canada,* June 1988, 107–113. Available online. URL: http://adsbit.harvard.edu/cgi-bin/nph-iarticle_query?bibcode=1988JRASC..82..107K. Accessed on January 29, 2005.

> Personal reminiscences of Reber by a fellow radio amateur who knew him well.

National Radio Astronomy Observatory. "The Discovery of Hydrogen Radio Emission by Ewen and Purcell." Available online. URL: http://www.nrao.edu/whatisra/hist_ewenpurcell.shtml. Accessed on February 2, 2005.

> Brief article recounting the 1951 discovery, which gave astronomers a new tool for mapping the Milky Way galaxy.

———. "Frequently Asked Questions about Radio Astronomy." Available online. URL: http://www.nrao.edu/whatisra/FAQ.shtml. Accessed on February 3, 2005.

> Answers questions that the public has asked, ranging from "What is radio astronomy?" to "What have you discovered lately?"

———. "How Radio Telescopes Work." Available online. URL: http://www.nrao.edu/whatisra/radiotel.shtml. Accessed on February 3, 2005.

> Article describing the basic features and operation of radio telescopes, as well as new techniques that have made the telescopes more sensitive and powerful.

Peratt, Anthony L. "In Memoriam: Grote Reber, 1911–2002, Founder of Radio Astronomy." *IEEE Transactions on Plasma Science* 3 (December 2003): 1,112–1,115. Available online. URL: http://

public.lanl.gov/alp/plasma/downloads/GroteReber.pdf. Accessed on February 5, 2005.

    Memorial article describes Reber's contributions to radio astronomy and related fields, focusing on Reber's research on long-wavelength radio waves in Tasmania.

————. "Prediction of 21-cm Line Radiation." Available online. URL: http:///www.gb.nrao.edu/fgdocs/HI21cm/21cm.html. Accessed on February 2, 2005.

    Short article describing Dutch astronomer Jan Oort's early recognition of radio astronomy's potential usefulness and the prediction of his student, H. C. Van de Hulst, that electrons in hydrogen atoms would give off radio waves 21 centimeters long.

Reber, Grote. "Cosmic Static." *Astrophysical Journal* 9 (June 1940): 621ff.

    One of several papers with this title that Reber published in various journals, this was the first paper describing extraterrestrial radio signals to appear in an astronomical journal. It inspired Dutch astronomers Jan Oort and Hendrick Van de Hulst to begin investigating the possibilities of radio astronomy.

————. "A Play Entitled the Beginning of Radio Astronomy." *Journal of the Royal Astronomical Society of Canada* 82 (June 1988): 93ff. Available online. URL: http://adsbit.harvard.edu/cgi-bin/nph-iarticle_query?bibcode=1988JRASC..82...93R. Accessed on January 29, 2005.

    Reber describes his own work and that of Karl Jansky in early radio astronomy.

Web Site

National Radio Astronomy Observatory. URL: http://www.nrao.edu. Accessed on February 4, 2005.

    Operated for the National Science Foundation by Associated Universities, Inc., the National Radio Astronomy Observatory has advanced radio telescopes at five sites worldwide. Its Web site includes a series of pages describing the science and history of radio astronomy.

COSMIC FIREWORKS

GEORGE GAMOW AND THE BIG BANG

Edwin Hubble established that galaxies were flying away from each other in all directions, like a crowd of people fleeing a disaster. But what were the galaxies fleeing? What had started their outward journey?

Hubble never suggested an answer to these questions, but other scientists did. In 1922, well before Hubble and Humason published their evidence that the universe was expanding, Alexander Friedmann, a Russian meteorologist (scientist who studies weather) and mathematician, suggested that the universe began with an explosion. Georges-Henri Lemaître, a Belgian astronomer, mathematician, and priest, independently proposed a similar idea in 1927.

Friedmann and Lemaître both based their conclusions on Einstein's general theory of relativity, which initially (until Einstein changed it in 1917) required the universe to be either expanding or contracting. Lemaître used Vesto Slipher's and Hubble's early measurements of redshifts in the spectra of galaxies to show that expansion was the more likely choice. Einstein's original theory led Friedmann and Lemaître to conclude that at some time in the distant past, all matter and energy in the universe had occupied a single point—what Einstein called a singularity. For unknown reasons, this point broke apart in what Lemaître called "fireworks of unimaginable beauty."

Few cosmologists knew of Lemaître's or Friedmann's work at first, and even fewer believed it. In the late 1940s and 1950s, however, Russian-born scientist George Gamow (pronounced GAM-off) made their theory widely known and physically testable and did perhaps more than any other person to bring about its acceptance. A man with a wide-ranging intellect, Gamow made important contributions to nuclear physics and genetics as well as to astronomy and cosmology. He was one of the first scientists to connect recent discoveries about the interior of atoms with ideas about the nature of stars and the beginning of the universe.

Quantum Genius

George Gamow was born Gyorgy Antonovich Gamow on March 4, 1904, in Odessa, then part of Russia (now in the Ukraine). His parents were teachers. Gamow showed an early interest in mathematics and science, which came to include astronomy after his father gave him a small telescope for his 13th birthday.

Russian-American scientist George Gamow, a pioneer in nuclear physics and genetics as well as astrophysics, popularized the idea that the universe began with the explosive expansion of a single, infinitely dense point. This proposal came to be known as the big bang theory. (George Washington University)

As a young man, Gamow studied mathematics at the Novorossia University in Odessa in 1922. In 1923, he transferred to the University of Leningrad (now the University of St. Petersburg), where his classes included physics and cosmology in addition to mathematics. He continued to study at the university until 1929 but may not have obtained a degree.

A summer program at the University of Göttingen, Germany, in 1928 introduced Gamow to the exciting discoveries being made in nuclear physics, including quantum mechanics, which describes the unique physical principles affecting atoms and subatomic particles such as electrons, protons, and neutrons. Gamow immediately applied his new knowledge to develop a theory explaining the breakdown of atoms that produces natural radioactivity. Quantum mechanics had previously been used to describe the structure of atoms, but Gamow was the first to apply it to the atomic nucleus.

Impressed by the young Russian, famed Danish physicist Niels Bohr arranged for Gamow to work at the Institute for Theoretical Physics, part of the University of Copenhagen in Denmark, in 1928 and 1929. Gamow's calculation of the energy needed to break up a nucleus by bombarding it with protons, made at this time, provided underpinnings for later scientists' work on nuclear fission (splitting) and fusion. He also began to develop theories about thermonuclear (atomic fusion) reactions inside the Sun and other stars. Some of his work was later used in developing the hydrogen bomb and in attempts to harness fusion energy for peaceful uses.

As a Rockefeller Fellow, Gamow spent the following year (1929–30) with Ernest Rutherford, another famous physicist, at the Cavendish Laboratory of Cambridge University in England. Under Rutherford's supervision, Gamow helped to develop an experiment that provided strong evidence for Albert Einstein's claim that matter (mass) and energy are equivalent. With this achievement added to his earlier ones, as Eamon Harper wrote in the spring 2000 issue of *GW Magazine,* George Gamow "established himself as one of the leaders in the . . . field of nuclear physics before his 25th birthday."

After Gamow spent a second year (1930–31) in Copenhagen, the government of the Soviet Union offered him a faculty post at the University of Leningrad and insisted that he return to Russia to accept it. Gamow taught physics at the university for several years, beginning in late 1931, but his mind was chiefly occupied with thinking of ways to escape the country. (In one of his failed attempts, he and his wife tried to paddle a rubber rowboat to freedom across the Black Sea.) Finally, he succeeded in arranging for both himself and his wife, Lyubov Vokhminzeva (whom he had married in 1931), to attend the International Solvay Congress on theoretical physics in Brussels, Belgium, in October 1933. They never returned to the Soviet Union.

From Atoms to Stars

Gamow stayed briefly at the Pierre Curie Institute in Paris and the University of London, then went to the United States in 1934. He joined the faculty of George Washington University in Washington, D.C., where he remained for most of his career. Gamow became a naturalized U.S. citizen in 1939.

During his first years at George Washington University, Gamow continued his work in nuclear physics. He and Hungarian-American physicist Edward Teller developed a theory describing beta decay, in which an atomic nucleus releases a high-speed electron (beta particle), in 1936. This was Gamow's last major contribution to pure nuclear physics.

Gamow then began applying his expertise in atomic physics to astronomy, a combination of fields that Eamon Harper says was "audacious in the extreme" at the time. Gamow and a few other astronomers had come to believe that the chemical elements were created by thermonuclear reactions in the superhot interiors of the Sun and other stars, but they were unsure how this could be accomplished. For one thing, the protons thought to make up stars' interiors had been expected to repel each other so strongly (because they all have the same electric charge) that they would be unable to fuse with one another, which would be required for them to form elements heavier than hydrogen. In his earlier explanation of natural radioactivity, however, Gamow had shown that, according to quantum mechanics, protons could "tunnel" through this electrical barrier often enough to permit fusion reactions.

In 1938 and 1939, Gamow inspired renowned German physicist Hans Bethe and American physicist Charles Critchfield, a former student of Gamow's, to propose a series of reactions through which the lightest elements (up to helium) might be formed inside stars. Gamow himself, meanwhile, described possible nuclear reactions in exploding stars called supernovas. In 1942, again working with Teller, Gamow also developed a theory that used some of his earlier ideas about nuclear physics to predict the internal structure of red giant stars.

Birth of the Elements

During the 1930s, geochemists drew on what they knew about the chemistry of Earth to work out what they believed to be the relative abundance of the elements in the universe. (Scientists had concluded that matter was distributed more or less evenly throughout the cosmos, so data from the Sun and nearby stars would also apply to more distant locations.) According to their figures, most matter was hydrogen or helium. All the heavier elements made up just 1 to 2 percent of the total.

Gamow wrote later in his memoir, *My World Line,* "It was natural to assume that the observed universal abundances of chemical elements do not result from the nucleosynthesis within the individual stars, which would lead to a great variety of chemical constitution." Instead, he concluded, at least some of the lightweight elements must have been born in the gigantic explosion that, like Friedmann and Lemaître, he believed had begun the expansion of the universe.

Gamow, along with these earlier scientists, believed that the universe at its origin was infinitely small, hot, and dense. At first, as all matter and energy—and space itself—began rushing away from this central point, only a tremendously hot soup of free electrons, protons, neutrons, and radiation existed. Gamow called this material the *ylem,* a Greek name for the formless substance out of which all elements were supposed to have been made; more recent scientists term it *plasma.* As the expansion continued, the *ylem* became thinner and cooler, allowing atomic nuclei and, later, complete atoms to form.

As a Ph.D. project, Gamow assigned one of his students, Ralph Asher Alpher, to work out the reactions by which the elements (at least the lightest ones, from hydrogen to lithium) could have been created from the *ylem.* Alpher was then to compare his predictions with what was known about the actual proportions of elements in the universe.

Alpher concluded that the first reaction to take place was the formation of deuterium (heavy hydrogen) nuclei from combinations of protons and neutrons. (A deuterium nucleus contains one proton and one neutron.) As the cooling continued, forms (isotopes) of the nuclei of helium and lithium followed. All these reactions took place in the first few minutes after the initial explosion. Alpher's predictions fit well with the known relative abundance of light elements, especially of helium, in the universe.

Gamow and Alpher presented Alpher's work in what became a famous paper, "The Origin of the Chemical Elements," published in the April 1, 1948, issue of *Physical Review*. Gamow, well known for his humor, could not resist adding Hans Bethe's name to the paper's author list, even though, according to most sources, Bethe had played no part in the research that the paper described. Doing so allowed Gamow to make an educated pun: He listed the paper's

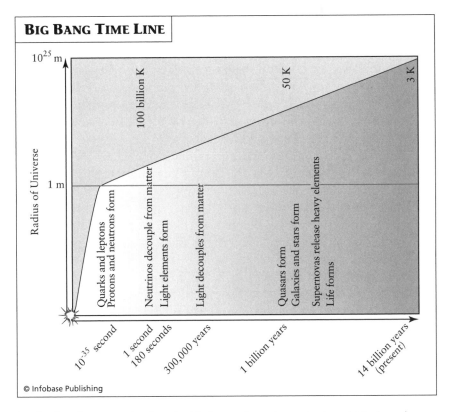

BIG BANG TIME LINE

© Infobase Publishing

In the first few seconds after the big bang, the universe is thought to have been an unbelievably hot soup of subatomic particles. Lightweight atomic nuclei appeared after about 180 seconds, but the soup took another 300,000 years to cool to the point where atoms could form. Once hydrogen atoms appeared, radiation separated from matter, and light flooded the universe. Quasars, galaxies, and stars began to form about a billion years after the big bang. Today— about 14 billion years after the universe began—the cosmic background radiation released by the big bang has cooled to three Kelvins.

authors as Alpher, Bethe, Gamow, which would be pronounced almost exactly like *alpha, beta, gamma,* the first three letters of the Greek alphabet.

Competing Theories

Gamow and Alpher's paper drew great attention to the explosion theory of the universe's origin. Not all cosmologists believed that such an explosion had occurred, however. Some favored a second explanation, which British astrophysicists Arthur Gold and Fred Hoyle and Austrian-born mathematician Hermann Bondi proposed in 1948, the same year that the Alpher-Bethe-Gamow paper was published. Bondi, Gold, and Hoyle said that the universe had had no beginning and would never end, but rather existed in what they called a steady state. They admitted that the universe was expanding, but they believed that the outward movement of the galaxies was balanced by spontaneous creation of new matter, which in turn formed galaxies to replace those speeding away.

Gamow and Hoyle were both good writers, able to explain their ideas to ordinary people as well as to scientists. Readers of the 1950s learned about the two men's dueling cosmology theories through books such as Hoyle's *The Nature of the Universe* (1950) and Gamow's *The Creation of the Universe* (1952). Gamow and Hoyle also spoke about their ideas on radio programs, and in one of these, a British Broadcasting Corporation (BBC) program aired in 1949, Hoyle gave the Lemaître-Gamow theory the name by which it is still known. Hoyle meant to make fun of the rival theory by calling it the "big bang idea," but people found the term so apt that it stuck.

A Testable Prediction

Many astronomers felt that the big bang and steady-state theories were about as hard to test as the religious creation myths that some skeptics said the theories resembled. In a short paper published in *Nature* in 1949, however, Ralph Asher Alpher and Robert Herman,

---

OTHER SCIENTISTS: FRED HOYLE

George Gamow and Fred Hoyle had opposing theories about the universe, but the two men were personally similar in many ways. Both were known for their lively sense of humor and fearless adoption of controversial ideas, for instance.

Hoyle was born in Bingley, Yorkshire, on June 24, 1915. He studied mathematics, nuclear physics (another interest he shared with Gamow), and eventually astronomy at Cambridge University, earning an M.A. in physics in 1939. He joined the Cambridge faculty in 1945 and remained there until retiring in 1972. He was knighted in that year and received the Crafoord Prize, considered equivalent to the Nobel Prize, in 1997. Hoyle died in Bournemouth, England, on August 20, 2001.

Hoyle did not change his mind easily. Even after new discoveries made most cosmologists abandon the steady-state theory in 1964, Hoyle continued to attack what he saw as the competing theory's weak points. Other scientists have since modified the big bang theory, in part by adapting some of Hoyle's ideas.

This was not the only time that Fred Hoyle and George Gamow discovered different parts of the same puzzle. Gamow, Ralph Asher Alpher, and Robert Herman worked out reactions by which the lightest chemical elements could have been created in the explosion that began the universe, but they could not explain the creation of heavier elements. Hoyle, with William Fowler and husband-and-wife astronomers Geoffrey and Margaret Burbidge, showed in a famous paper published in 1957, "Synthesis of the Elements in Stars," that these elements were created in the explosive death of stars called supernovas.

Also like Gamow, Fred Hoyle was a well-known popularizer of science. Hoyle's books for nonscientists included *The Nature of the Universe* (1950), which described the steady-state theory, and *Frontiers of Astronomy* (1955). He also wrote best-selling science fiction novels such as *The Black Cloud* (1957).

---

following up an idea of Gamow's, suggested a way in which the big bang theory could be proved, or at least strongly supported.

Alpher and Herman theorized that the big bang released not only matter but also electromagnetic radiation, in the form of particles called photons. The radiation, like the matter, cooled slowly as it traveled outward. The photons spread within the expanding cloud of subatomic particles, yet the radiation could not escape the fog of hydrogen nuclei until the cloud cooled enough for electrons to begin attaching themselves to protons, forming the first hydrogen atoms. The radiation then broke free of the cloud and sailed out into space in all directions, making the universe transparent for the first time.

The two cosmologists claimed that at that time, about 300,000 years after the original explosion, the radiation would have cooled to a temperature of about five kelvins (K), or five degrees above absolute zero (450 degrees below zero degrees Fahrenheit). The redshift caused by outward movement, meanwhile, would have pushed the radiation from the wavelengths associated with light to the longer wavelengths called microwaves, part of the radio area of the electromagnetic spectrum. Alpher and Herman said that detecting this radiation and showing that it had the characteristics they predicted would provide powerful evidence that the big bang theory was correct.

Most astronomers did not find Alpher and Herman's proposal very helpful. Searching for the radiation the two men described would require radio telescopes, and at the time, such telescopes had not advanced much beyond Grote Reber's backyard dish. Radio astronomy advanced greatly during the 1950s, but by then, Alpher and Herman's idea had been forgotten.

Echoes of the Big Bang

In the early 1960s, Princeton University radio astronomer Robert Dicke independently reached the same conclusion that Alpher and Herman had. Dicke and several colleagues began building an antenna to search for the predicted microwave radiation. Before their antenna was complete, however, they learned in late 1964 that Arno Penzias and Robert W. Wilson, two radio astronomers at Bell Laboratories in Holmdel, New Jersey, had already found the radiation by accident.

In his memoir, *My World Line,* George Gamow understatedly called Penzias and Wilson's discovery "a pleasant surprise." As

Alpher and Herman had predicted, the microwave radiation proved to be equally strong in every part of the sky. It was also close to the temperature that the two earlier scientists had suggested—about 3.5 K, rather than the 5 K that Herman and Alpher had named—and had other features that they had described. The discovery of this cosmic microwave background radiation convinced most cosmologists that the big bang theory was basically correct. This radiation's existence remains the strongest evidence in favor of the theory.

Bell Laboratories radio astronomers Arno Penzias (left) and Robert Wilson stand in front of the antenna with which they detected cosmic background radiation, the echo of the big bang, in 1964. (Lucent Technologies Inc./Bell Labs)

A Wide-Ranging Intellect

George Gamow's mind was too restless to confine itself to any one area of science. He turned from astronomy to genetics in 1953, soon after James Watson and Francis Crick published their landmark paper describing the molecular structure of the genetic material, DNA (deoxyribonucleic acid). Gamow was the first to suggest, in a letter to Crick written in mid-1953, that DNA molecules would prove to contain a "genetic code" that carried instructions for making proteins, a large class of chemicals that do most of the work in cells. Gamow's basic ideas about the code's structure were later shown to be correct.

During the 1950s, Gamow also continued his writing of popular books about science, which he had begun with *Mr. Tompkins in Wonderland*, published in 1939. His best-known books for nonscientists include *The Birth and Death of the Sun* (1940) and *One, Two, Three . . . Infinity* (1947). The United Nations Educational,

PARALLELS: TWO ACCIDENTAL DISCOVERIES

The discovery of the cosmic background radiation by Arno Allen Penzias (born in Germany in 1933) and Robert Woodrow Wilson (born in 1936 in Houston, Texas) was similar in many ways to the discovery that founded radio astronomy—Karl Jansky's detection of radio waves coming from the Milky Way in the 1930s.

Penzias and Wilson, like Jansky, worked for Bell Laboratories in Holmdel, New Jersey. Also like Jansky, the later researchers did not set out to look for signals from space. The antenna they were using had been designed to detect broadcasts from early communication satellites. It was no longer needed for that purpose, so they were modifying it for radio astronomy.

In the course of this work, Penzias and Wilson tried to find the sources of signals that might interfere with the antenna's function as a radio telescope. Like Karl Jansky, they identified several types of interference but were left with a steady, low-level hiss that they could not explain. They eliminated possibilities such as equipment error, radio signals from New York City, and even echoes produced by the droppings of pigeons that had nested in the 20-foot (6-m), horn-shaped antenna.

Penzias and Wilson's hiss remained as much a mystery as Jansky's had been, until a colleague suggested that they contact Robert Dicke at Princeton. After visiting Holmdel and looking over the two Bell scientists' data, Dicke realized that they had found the cosmic background radiation he had been preparing to seek. (According to a Public Broadcasting System article, Dicke returned to Princeton and sadly told his research group, "We've been scooped.") In two adjacent papers published in the July 1, 1965, *Astrophysical Journal,* Penzias and Wilson described the radiation they detected, and Dicke's team explained the radiation's significance in terms of the big bang. Penzias and Wilson won shares of the Nobel Prize in physics for their discovery in 1978.

Scientific and Cultural Organization (UNESCO) awarded Gamow the Kalinga Prize for popularization of science in 1956.

Gamow was elected to numerous scientific societies, including the U.S. National Academy of Sciences (1953). He left George

Washington University in 1956 and moved to the University of Colorado, Boulder, where he spent the rest of his career. He also divorced his wife at this time. In 1958, he married Barbara Perkins, a former publicity manager for Cambridge University Press, which had published many of his popular books. Gamow died, probably from liver disease, at age 64 in Boulder on August 19, 1968.

With his wide-ranging interests in many scientific fields, George Gamow provided, according to mathematician Stanislaw Ulam (quoted by Eamon Harper), "perhaps the last example of amateurism in scientific work on a grand scale." Harper also quotes Edward Teller as saying that Gamow "was fantastic in his ideas. He was right, he was wrong. More often wrong than right. Always interesting; . . . and when his idea was not wrong it was not only right, it was new."

Chronology

1904	Gyorgy Antonovich Gamow born in Odessa, Russia, on March 4
1922	Alexander Friedmann concludes on the basis of Einstein's general theory of relativity that all matter and energy originated in an infinitely small point
1923	Gamow begins attending University of Leningrad
1927	Georges-Henri Lemaître proposes that the universe began with the explosion of a primeval atom
1928	Gamow learns about nuclear physics in Göttingen, Germany, and uses quantum mechanics to explain radioactivity
1928–29	Gamow attends the Institute for Theoretical Physics in Copenhagen, Denmark, calculates energy required to split atomic nucleus, and develops theories about fusion reactions in stars
1929–30	Gamow works under Ernest Rutherford at Cavendish Laboratory in Cambridge University, England

1930–31	Gamow spends a second year at Institute for Theoretical Physics
1931	Gamow begins teaching at University of Leningrad and marries Lyubov Vokhminzeva
1933	Gamow defects from Soviet Union with his wife in October
1934	Gamow moves to United States and joins faculty of George Washington University
1936	Gamow develops theory of beta decay with Edward Teller
1938–39	Inspired by Gamow, Hans Bethe and Charles Critchfield work out nuclear reactions by which lightweight elements could be created in stars; Gamow describes nuclear reactions in supernovas and publishes his first popular science book, *Mr. Tompkins in Wonderland*
1942	Gamow and Edward Teller use nuclear physics to predict structure of red giant stars
1947–48	With Gamow, Ralph Asher Alpher works out sequence of events that could have formed atomic nuclei of lightweight elements in the first few minutes after the explosion that began the expansion of the universe
1948	Hermann Bondi, Arthur Gold, and Fred Hoyle present steady-state theory; paper describing Alpher's research, "The Origin of the Chemical Elements," published in April 1st *Physical Review*
1949	In a radio broadcast, Fred Hoyle coins the term *big bang* to describe the theory that the universe originated in a primordial explosion; Ralph Asher Alpher and Robert Herman propose that microwave radiation released in the big bang might be detected
1953	Gamow proposes that DNA contains a "genetic code" that carries instructions for making proteins; he is elected to U.S. National Academy of Sciences
1956	Gamow moves to University of Colorado, Boulder, divorces his first wife, and wins UNESCO's Kalinga Prize for popularization of science

1958	Gamow marries Barbara Perkins
1964	Arno Penzias and Robert Wilson detect cosmic microwave background radiation, providing strong support for the big bang theory
1968	Gamow dies in Boulder, Colorado, on August 19

Further Reading

Books

Bartusiak, Marcia, ed. *Archives of the Universe: A Treasury of Astronomy's Historic Works of Discovery.* New York: Pantheon, 2004.
Includes excerpts from famous scientific papers related to the development of the big bang theory and commentary describing their history and importance.

Ferris, Timothy. *Coming of Age in the Milky Way.* New York: William Morrow, 1988.
History of humankind's attempts to understand the nature of the universe; includes material on George Gamow and the big bang theory.

Gamow, George. *The Creation of the Universe.* New York: Viking, 1952.
Describes Gamow's version of the big bang theory.

———. *My World Line: An Informal Autobiography.* New York: Viking Press, 1970.
Concentrates on Gamow's youth in Russia and Europe, including his defection from the Soviet Union; provides limited information about his life in the United States.

Hoyle, Fred. *The Nature of the Universe.* New York: Harper, 1950.
Describes the steady-state theory of the universe, a rival to the big bang theory that Hoyle, Arthur Gold, and Hermann Bondi developed in 1948.

Articles

Alpher, Ralph Asher, Hans Bethe, and George Gamow. "The Origin of the Chemical Elements." *Physical Review* 7 (April 1, 1948): 803ff.

Classic paper describing how lightweight chemical elements might have formed shortly after the gigantic explosion that began the universe.

Harper, Eamon. "Getting a Bang out of Gamow." *GW Magazine*, spring 2000. Available online. URL: http://www.gwu.edu/~physics/gwmageh.htm. Accessed on September 26, 2005.
Article describes Gamow's years at George Washington University, during which he made most of his important discoveries.

LaRocco, Chris, and Blair Rothstein. "The Big Bang: It Sure Was BIG!!" University of Michigan Web site. Available online. URL: http://www.umich.edu/~gs265/bigbang.htm. Accessed on September 26, 2005.
Clear explanation of the big bang theory of the universe's origin as cosmologists see it today, including evidence that supports the theory and ongoing questions.

NASA WMAP Web site. "Tests of the Big Bang: The CMB." Available online. URL: http://map.gsfc.nasa.gov/m_uni/uni_101bbtest3.html. Accessed on September 26, 2005.
Describes the discovery and nature of the cosmic microwave background, its importance for understanding the origin of the universe, and current research aimed at learning more about it.

WGBH (PBS) Web site. "Penzias and Wilson Discover Cosmic Microwave Radiation 1965." Available online. URL: http://www.pbs.org/wgbh/aso/databank/entries/dp65co.html. Accessed on February 4, 2005.
Describes Arno Penzias and Robert Wilson's accidental discovery of evidence that supports the big bang theory.

Web Site

The George Gamow Memorial Lecture Series at the University of Colorado at Boulder. URL: http://www.colorado.edu/physics/Web/Gamow. Accessed on February 1, 2005.
This site, sponsored by the university's physics department, includes chronologies of Gamow's life and career and a list of his most important writings.

5

IS ANYONE OUT THERE?

FRANK DRAKE AND THE SEARCH FOR EXTRATERRESTRIAL INTELLIGENCE

Since ancient times, people have wondered whether life existed on other planets or in other star systems. For instance, the Greek philosopher Metrodorus wrote in the fourth century B.C. that "to consider the Earth as the only populated world in infinite space is as absurd as to assert that in an entire field of millet [a type of grain], only one grain will grow." Much later, as telescopes improved, a few astronomers even thought they saw evidence of such life. In 1877, Italian astronomer Giovanni Schiaparelli reported that he saw "canals" on the planet Mars, and about 15 years later, Percival Lowell, an American astronomer, claimed that he had spotted not only Schiaparelli's canals but also the vegetation around them. These observations were shown to be mistaken, however. Few scientists

Frank Drake made the first search for radio signals from extraterrestrial civilizations in 1960, about the time this photograph was taken. (National Radio Astronomy Observatory/AUI/NSF)

in the early 20th century thought that life could exist beyond Earth or, if it did, that human beings would ever be able to detect it.

That is no longer true. Although still a minority among astronomers, scientists with substantial reputations now scan the sky for radio or other signals from intelligent beings in distant star systems. The Search for Extraterrestrial Intelligence, or SETI, has drawn support from the National Aeronautics and Space Administration (NASA), private foundations, and even millions of ordinary computer users who donate their machines' idle processing power to the hunt. The man most responsible for this change of attitude is radio astronomer Frank D. Drake.

Dreaming of Intelligent Life

Frank Drake has said that he began wondering whether intelligent beings might live on other planets when he was just eight years old. He was born on May 28, 1930, in Chicago to Richard Drake, a chemical engineer, and Winifred Thompson Drake. Visits to Chicago's Museum of Science and Industry and the Adler Planetarium inspired him as a child, and he and his best friend liked to play with motors, radios, and chemistry sets.

Supported by an ROTC (Reserve Officers' Training Corps) scholarship, Drake enrolled in Cornell University, in Ithaca, New York, in 1949 to study aircraft design. He soon became more interested in electronics, however, and changed his major to engineering physics. In his junior year, he heard Otto Struve, a well-known astrophysicist, say in a lecture that half the stars in the galaxy might have planetary systems, and some of those planets might well contain life. "It was an electric moment," Drake wrote in his autobiography, *Is Anyone Out There?* "I wasn't alone anymore. . . . This most preeminent astronomer . . . dared to speak aloud what I had only dreamed about."

Drake earned his B.A. from Cornell in 1952, then worked for the U.S. Navy for three years as a shipboard electronics officer to pay back his scholarship. In 1955, when his military commitment was completed, he began graduate studies at Harvard. He had intended to study optical astronomy, but a summer job as a radio astronomer interested him in that branch of astronomy instead. After earning his Ph.D. in 1958, Drake joined the newly established National Radio Astronomy Observatory (NRAO) in Green Bank, West Virginia. He immediately began making important discoveries, including finding belts of radiation around Jupiter similar to those detected around Earth.

Searching for Radio Signals

Drake had concluded while still at Harvard that radio waves would be the most economical form of electromagnetic radiation to use in sending messages across interstellar distances. The ideal tool for detecting such messages, therefore, would be a radio telescope. In spring 1959, at first just for fun, he calculated the maximum distance from which NRAO's new 85-foot (25.9-m) telescope might detect radio signals as powerful as the strongest signals generated on Earth. He arrived at a figure of 12 light-years. Several stars similar to the Sun lay within this distance, so Drake and several other NRAO astronomers began planning a project to look for signals that might come from intelligent beings on planets circling these stars. Such signals, Drake thought, would have a very narrow bandwidth, regular repetition, and other features that would make them easy to distinguish from natural radio signals.

In September of that same year, Drake and the other astronomers were startled to read an article called "Searching for Interstellar Communications" in the respected science journal *Nature*. Philip Morrison and Giuseppe Cocconi, the two Cornell physicists who had written the article, proposed using radio telescopes to look for signals from extraterrestrial civilizations, just as Drake hoped to do. They recommended searching on the 21-centimeter (about 8-in.) wavelength, the microwave radio band on which single atoms of hydrogen send out natural signals. They pointed out that hydrogen is the most abundant element in the universe, making its wavelength a logical choice for communication. The Cornell scientists' article "made us feel good because now there were further arguments for what we were doing," Drake wrote in a memoir published in *Cosmic*

Search, an early magazine devoted to SETI research. NRAO's director gave Drake's group permission to go ahead with their project.

Project Ozma

Drake called his investigation Project Ozma, after the princess who ruled the land of Oz in L. Frank Baum's fantasy novels. He wrote in *Is Anyone Out There?* that he chose that name because his imagined home of extraterrestrial civilizations, like Oz, was "a land far away, difficult to reach, and populated by strange and exotic beings."

Project Ozma began in the chilly predawn hours of April 8, 1960, and continued for the next two months. Besides the telescope, Drake used a narrow-band radio receiver tuned to the hydrogen wavelength and a new device called a parametric amplifier, which greatly increased sensitivity to signals without increasing noise (interference). He looked for signals from two nearby Sun-like stars, Tau Ceti and Epsilon Eridani.

Except for one strong signal that proved to come from a passing plane, Drake's project detected nothing unusual. Nonetheless, he saw Project Ozma as a historic effort, the first serious search for intelligent extraterrestrial life—a quest he was sure would take decades, perhaps even centuries. Drake wrote in *Is Anyone Out There?* that Project Ozma "portrayed SETI to other scientists and to the world at large for the first time as a legitimate and doable scientific endeavor."

The Drake Equation

In November 1961, Drake and J. Peter Pearman, an officer on the National Academy of Sciences' Space Science Board, called together the first conference on what became known as SETI. At the conference, held at NRAO, Drake presented an equation that has since become famous:

$$N = R \, f_p \, n_e \, f_l \, f_i \, f_c \, L$$

Drake's equation was designed to determine N, the number of detectable civilizations in space. N, Drake concluded, is the product of the rate of star formation (R), the fraction of stars that form planets (f_p), the number of planets hospitable to life (n_e), the fraction of those planets on which life actually develops (f_l), the fraction of planets where life evolves into intelligent beings (f_i), the fraction of planets with intelligent creatures capable of interstellar communication (f_c), and the average length of time that such a civilization remains detectable (L). The members of the SETI conference discussed possible values for the variables in the equation and concluded that between 1,000 and 100 million advanced civilizations were likely to exist in the Milky Way. In *Is Anyone Out There?*, published in 1992, Drake put the number at about 10,000 civilizations.

Drake's equation provided a framework for thinking about SETI that researchers in the field still use. With its many lettered variables, the equation looks satisfyingly precise. Critics at the time and since, however, have pointed out that the values of the variables, except for R and perhaps f_p, were—and still are—completely unknown. Without numbers to plug into it, the critics say, the Drake equation essentially means nothing.

Establishing a Career

Only 10 scientists attended Drake's conference. Drake realized that few astronomers were willing to risk their jobs by publicly supporting what seemed to be an impractical, if not completely unscientific, effort. He saw that he needed to focus on less controversial subjects if he wanted to continue his career in radio astronomy. During the early 1960s, therefore, he studied radio emissions from Venus. He proved that heat caused the planet's signals and calculated that Venus had a surface temperature of about 890°F (477°C), much higher than most astronomers had thought. Space probes later confirmed this figure.

Drake joined Cornell University in 1964 as associate director of the university's Center for Radiophysics and Space Research, a position he held until 1975. Two years later, he became the

Issues: Are We Alone?

From Metrodorus to Frank Drake, supporters of the idea that other intelligent life-forms must exist in the universe have based their belief on the idea that there are so many stars in the cosmos that surely, among them all, some besides our Sun must have planets on which the right conditions for life exist. Indirect support for this idea began appearing in the late 1990s, when several groups of astronomers found evidence that certain other stars do in fact have planets. Biologists on Earth have also discovered living things thriving in conditions that would not have been expected to sustain life. For instance, whole ecosystems have developed around vents spewing gas and hot water on the deep-sea floor, far from oxygen and sunlight. High temperatures and chemicals that would poison most living things do not harm these creatures.

However, not all scientists agree that life—let alone intelligent life—is likely to have arisen in other planetary systems. Renowned evolutionary biologist Ernst Mayr told *Time* reporter Frederic Golden in 2000, "The chance that this improbable phenomenon [the creation of life] could have occurred several times is exceedingly small, no matter how many millions of planets in the universe." Similarly, paleontologist Peter Ward and astronomer Donald Brownlee concluded in *Rare Earth,* a book published in 2000, that although simple life-forms such as microorganisms may have appeared on other planets, complex life is rare. High temperatures, harsh radiation, and collisions with comets or asteroids usually would have destroyed living things before they could develop very far. Ward and Brownlee maintain that conscious, intelligent life may be unique to Earth.

director of Cornell's new Arecibo Ionospheric Observatory. The Arecibo Telescope, located in Puerto Rico, is still the largest single-dish radio telescope in the world.

After two years at Arecibo, Drake returned to the United States in 1968 to take over the chairmanship of the Cornell astronomy department. He was director of the National Astronomy and Ionosphere Center, which managed the Arecibo Observatory, from 1970 to

1981. From 1976 to 1984, he was the Goldwin Smith Professor of Astronomy at Cornell.

The *Pioneer* Plaque

Drake had no time to look for incoming messages from space during his Cornell years, but in the 1970s, he had several chances to send outgoing ones. First, in 1972, he worked with Carl Sagan, an astronomer and well-known popularizer of science as well as a fellow believer in SETI, to design a plaque that would be placed aboard NASA's *Pioneer 10* unmanned spacecraft. The main purpose of the craft was to send back pictures of Jupiter and its moons, but *Pioneer*'s swing near that giant planet also would ultimately fling it out of the solar system. *Pioneer 10* was the first spacecraft expected to enter deep space.

Drake and Sagan had known each other since Drake's days at NRAO, when the two had corresponded about Drake's work on the temperature of Venus. In December 1969, Sagan, who had been working with NASA on the Pioneer Project, told Drake excitedly that the agency had approved placing a message on the craft for possible extrasolar civilizations to find. The message would be an engraving on a small aluminum plaque. Sagan asked Drake to help him decide what the engraving should show, and Drake was happy to agree.

Sagan and Drake worked out a design featuring a naked man and woman standing in front of the *Pioneer* spacecraft. Their proposed picture also included a map of the solar system, showing the spacecraft leaving from Earth, and a second map picturing Earth's location within the Milky Way galaxy. Using their specifications, Sagan's wife, Linda, made the line drawing from which the engraving would be produced.

When NASA released pictures of the plaque at the time of *Pioneer 10*'s launch on March 2, 1972, some people criticized the design because it showed nude humans. Drake and Sagan welcomed the controversy, however, because it brought wide publicity to their attempt to communicate with extraterrestrial civilizations. A second plaque, engraved with the same design, was placed aboard *Pioneer 11,* a similar spacecraft launched on April 5, 1973.

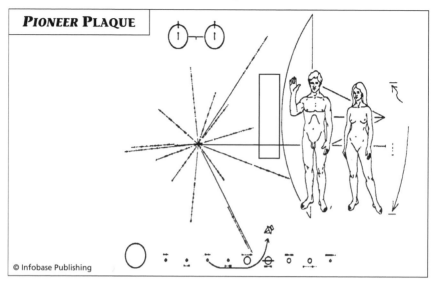

Carl Sagan and Frank Drake designed this engraved plaque, which was placed aboard the Pioneer 10 *and* Pioneer 11 *spacecraft in the early 1970s. These spacecraft were the first ones intended to leave the solar system, and the plaques were the first deliberate attempt to send a message to extraterrestrial civilizations. The plaque includes male and female humans standing in front of the spacecraft, a picture of the solar system showing the spacecraft leaving Earth, and a map showing distances from Earth to nearby pulsars.*

More Messages to the Stars

Drake had a second opportunity to send a message to extraterrestrial civilizations during the dedication of improvements to his own Arecibo Observatory on November 16, 1974. As part of the dedication ceremony, the observatory broadcast a three-minute radio signal toward the Great Cluster in the constellation of Hercules, a group of at least 300,000 stars about 25,000 light-years away. This was the first outgoing radio signal deliberately intended for extraterrestrial communication.

Drake designed the Arecibo message, which was encoded in the binary counting system. This system shows all numbers in the form of 1s and 0s, or "on" and "off" pulses. The message included diagrams of the five molecules needed for life on Earth (hydrogen, carbon, nitrogen, oxygen, and phosphorus); chemical formulas for the components of DNA, the genetic material of Earthly life, and a picture of the DNA molecule's double helix (corkscrew-like) structure; a map of the solar system; and simplified figures of a human and a radio telescope.

Finally, in 1977, Drake worked with Carl Sagan, among others, to design a second interstellar communication for NASA. This time the communication was a copper phonograph record, placed aboard the spacecraft *Voyager 1* and *Voyager 2*. The record's aluminum cover was engraved with pictures showing how to set up an

---

ISSUES: WILL ALIENS VISIT EARTH?

After Frank Drake broadcast the Arecibo message in 1974, Sir Martin Ryle, the Astronomer Royal (chief astronomer) of England, criticized Drake for revealing humanity's existence to extraterrestrial civilizations. Ryle feared that by doing so, Drake might have put Earth at risk of alien invasion.

Drake replied that he considered visits from extraterrestrial civilizations—threatening or otherwise—to be very unlikely. He also pointed out that it was far too late to try to keep human existence secret. Television signals carry far into space, so humanity began sending unintentional messages to the stars when TV programs were first broadcast in the 1950s. Aliens, he said, might obtain their first glimpses of Earth by watching *I Love Lucy* or *Howdy Doody*.

Drake has often said that, even for civilizations far more advanced than that of human beings, interstellar travel would waste too much energy and time to be worth undertaking. Most stars, he notes, are thousands or millions of light-years away. Even if a starship could travel at almost the speed of light, it would take millennia to make the journey. For this reason, Drake does not share the common belief that so-called unidentified flying objects (UFOs) are spacecraft from alien civilizations. "It doesn't pay to transport *things* through space as long as they [extraterrestrial civilizations] can transport *information*," he wrote in *Is Anyone Out There?*

attached player (cartridge and needle). The cover also carried some of the same types of diagrams that had appeared on the *Pioneer* plaque—but no nude people.

The record itself contained an hour and a half of recorded music from a variety of cultures, spoken greetings in 60 languages, sounds of Earth ranging from a human heartbeat to the song of a humpback whale and the roar of thunder, and 115 encoded television images of scenes from around the world. Among the speakers on the record was then–U.S. president Jimmy Carter, who said, "This is a present from a small distant world, a token of our sounds, our science, our images, our music, our thoughts, and our feelings. We are attempting to survive our time so we may live into yours. We hope someday, having solved the problems we face, to join a community of galactic civilizations. This record represents . . . our goodwill in a vast and awesome universe."

From Golden Fleece to National Goal

Except for the *Pioneer* plaque and the *Voyager* record, NASA showed little interest in attempts to communicate with extraterrestrial civilizations during the 1960s and 1970s. A few SETI projects funded by other sources took place during these years, however. The Soviet Union sponsored numerous SETI attempts in the 1960s, for instance. Universities and the Planetary Society, an organization that Carl Sagan founded in 1979 to support space projects that the government did not wish to pay for, sponsored several SETI projects in the United States in the 1970s.

Congress was even less receptive to SETI projects than NASA was. A low point in congressional attitude came on February 16, 1978, when Wisconsin senator William Proxmire gave a NASA SETI proposal one of his notorious Golden Fleece Awards. Proxmire assigned these so-called awards to government projects that he considered a waste of money. Worse still, in 1982, Proxmire persuaded Congress to pass an amendment blocking all funding for future SETI projects.

Better times lay ahead, however. First, during an hour-long conversation, Carl Sagan persuaded Proxmire to drop his objections to

SETI funding. As a result, limited funds were restored to NASA's SETI programs in 1983.

Sagan also drafted a letter supporting SETI projects and convinced 72 other scientists, including seven Nobel Prize winners, to sign it. The letter was published in the highly regarded American journal *Science* on October 29, 1982. At about the same time, a committee of the prestigious National Research Council, part of the National Academy of Sciences, recommended that SETI be established as a national goal.

Frank Drake, meanwhile, decided to devote a larger part of his own time to SETI. In November 1984, he founded the SETI Institute, a private research organization devoted entirely to the goal of contacting extraterrestrial civilizations, in Mountain View, California. Drake was the institute's president for many years and, later, was chairman of its board of trustees.

Also in 1984, Drake joined the faculty of the University of California, Santa Cruz (UCSC), where he taught astronomy and astrophysics. Drake was UCSC's dean of natural sciences from 1984 to 1988 and acting associate vice chancellor for university advancement in 1989 and 1990.

Rising from the Ashes

After years of planning, NASA began work on a major SETI project in 1988. The project was expected to last throughout the 1990s. It would include both a "targeted search" of 1,000 stars that SETI scientists thought likely to have planets and an "all-sky survey" that would repeatedly scan the whole volume of deep space for signals on any of a wide variety of wavelengths. The project planned to employ more than a hundred people and obtain data from radio telescopes in California, West Virginia, Puerto Rico, France, and Australia.

Unfortunately for Drake and other SETI enthusiasts, Congress canceled the NASA project's funding on September 22, 1993. Refusing to give up, Drake and the others turned to private donors, just as George Ellery Hale had done for his big telescopes a century before. Like Hale, they were successful, persuading foundations and wealthy individuals such as Microsoft cofounder Paul Allen to give a total of $7.5 million to keep the former NASA project alive.

The targeted search portion of NASA SETI, renamed Project Phoenix after the mythical bird that was reborn from the ashes of its own fiery death, began observing again in February 1995. The system used radio telescopes at Arecibo, Green Bank, and New South Wales, Australia, to scan about 700 nearby Sun-type stars. Drake said in 1997 that the

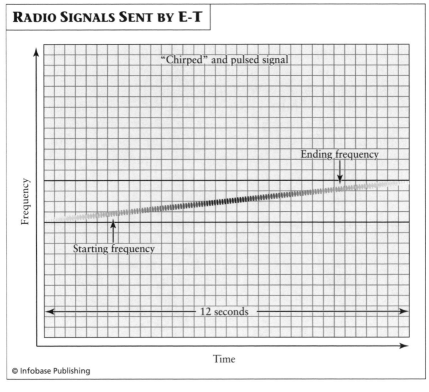

© Infobase Publishing

Radio signals sent deliberately by extraterrestrial civilizations are likely to be different from natural radio signals in several ways. Intentional signals will probably be narrow in bandwidth (consisting of waves that all have about the same length); they will most likely be pulsed (turning rapidly on and off) rather than continuous; and because they will come from a planet moving around a star, Doppler shifting will make them change slightly in frequency, or "chirp," during a short observation period.

instrumentation used by Project Phoenix at that time was 100 trillion times as sensitive as the equipment he had employed in Project Ozma.

   Drake and other SETI enthusiasts were encouraged when astronomers such as Geoffrey Marcy and Paul Butler began finding evidence in the mid-1990s that some other stars in fact did have planets, even though the planets seemed unlikely to contain life. They were also heartened by popular support for SETI projects.

SOLVING PROBLEMS: SETI@HOME

Searching for a deliberate extraterrestrial signal amid all the radio noise in the universe is, as Frank Drake wrote in *Is Anyone Out There?*, "like hunting for a needle in a cosmic haystack of inconceivable size." Looking for strong signals in a limited range of radio wavelengths is not too difficult, but the task becomes almost impossible when the search is extended to weak signals and a wide variety of frequencies. "It would take a monstrous supercomputer to get the job done," Ron Hipschman writes in "How SETI@home Works," an article on the SETI@home Web site.

   SETI research groups could never afford such a computer. Fortunately, Hipschman says, "the data analysis task can be easily broken up into little pieces that can all be worked on separately and in parallel." In the late 1990s, the SETI team at the University of California, Berkeley, realized that the work of analyzing the mountains of data from Arecibo could be parceled out among millions of ordinary home computers. That is the purpose of SETI@home.

   A computer user wishing to take part in SETI@home downloads software from the program's Web site and installs it on the computer. The software, in turn, periodically downloads a segment of Arecibo data from the Web site. When the computer is turned on but is not being used by its owner, the software turns on and begins analyzing the data. The user can regain control of the computer at any time, leaving the SETI analysis to be continued later. When the analysis is complete, the results are uploaded to the Web site, where they are merged into a large database and checked against known sources of radio interference. Another unit of data is then sent to the home computer.

In May 1999, for instance, the University of California, Berkeley, released screen-saver software called SETI@home, which allowed computer users to apply their machines' idle processing time to analysis of radio signals collected by the Arecibo Telescope. Almost 2 million people downloaded the software within a year.

The Father of SETI

Project Phoenix ended in March 2004, but the SETI Institute is working on or planning several new projects. One, called the Allen Telescope Array in honor of Paul Allen, who provided half of its initial funding, will set up several hundred 20-foot (6.1-m) radio

Currently being constructed in Northern California, the Allen Telescope Array will eventually consist of 350 antennas such as these, each 20 feet (6 m) in diameter. The advantages of this array for SETI are its ability to be used full time for the search and to "zero-in" on several star systems at once. It will also be an extremely powerful instrument for conventional radio astronomical research. (Seth Shostak/SETI Institute)

telescopes at the University of California (Berkeley) observatory in Hat Creek, California. The dishes can be steered as a unit, as if they were a single giant telescope. They will be used both for SETI research and for standard radio astronomy projects carried out by the university. The first group of dishes in the array is scheduled to go into operation in 2006. The SETI Institute and the Planetary Society are also sponsoring several optical SETI projects, which will look for artificial light signals.

Frank Drake, meanwhile, continues to be a spokesperson for SETI, which he still believes, as he wrote in 1992, "promises answers to our most profound questions about who we are and where we stand in the universe." He retired from the University of Santa Cruz in 1996, but he is still an emeritus professor there, as well as a trustee of the SETI Institute and a director of its Center for SETI Research. He is a member of the National Academy of Sciences, the American Academy of Arts and Sciences, and many other scientific societies, and in recent years, he has won several awards. In 1999, for example, the NRAO chose Drake to give the annual Jansky Lecture, an honor given to scientists who make significant contributions to the study of cosmic radio waves.

Drake sees far beyond today's earthbound SETI attempts. For instance, he hopes that someday an Arecibo-type radio telescope will be built in Crater Saha, on the dark side of the Moon. Because the Moon always turns the same side toward the Earth, he points out, the opposite side is shielded from interfering radio signals from the planet. A radio telescope built there could receive a full range of signals, including wavelengths blocked by Earth's atmosphere. Such a telescope could be much larger than any on Earth because the Moon has less gravity to weigh down and deform the telescope's materials. The Moon also lacks wind, which can change the shape of telescope mirrors and other equipment.

In 1997, UCSC reporter Jessica Gorman quoted Seth Shostak, a SETI Institute scientist, as saying that Drake "is the father of SETI. . . . He's kind of the Lewis and Clark of finding our cosmic cousins." Lawrence Squeri, professor of history at East Stroudsburg University in Pennsylvania, wrote in 2004, "If extraterrestrial intelligences are finally encountered, future historians will note that Frank Drake was the pioneer."

Chronology

fourth century B.C.	Greek philosopher Metrodorus writes that life is likely to exist in many parts of the universe
1877	Italian astronomer Giovanni Schiaparelli claims to see canals on Mars
1890s	American astronomer Percival Lowell describes supposed Martian canals in more detail
1930	Frank D. Drake born in Chicago on May 28
1952	Drake earns B.A. in engineering physics from Cornell University
1952–55	Drake works as shipboard electronics officer for U.S. Navy
1955	A summer job in radio astronomy convinces Drake to change to that field
1958	Drake earns Ph.D. in radio astronomy from Harvard University, joins the National Radio Astronomy Observatory (NRAO) in Green Bank, West Virginia, and finds belts of radiation around Jupiter
1959	In spring, Drake begins planning to use an 85-foot (25.5-m) NRAO telescope to look for radio signals from nearby stars
1960	Project Ozma begins on April 8 and ends in late May without detecting any extraterrestrial signals
1960s	Soviet Union conducts numerous SETI projects; early in the decade, Drake calculates surface temperature of Venus
1961	First conference on SETI held at NRAO in November, during which Drake presents an equation for calculating the number of detectable civilizations in space
1964	Drake becomes associate director of Cornell University's Center for Radiophysics and Space Research
1966	Drake becomes director of Arecibo Ionospheric Observatory in Puerto Rico, managed by Cornell

1968	Drake returns to Cornell's New York campus and becomes chairman of university's astronomy department
1969	In December, Drake and Carl Sagan design engraved message for extraterrestrial civilizations to be placed aboard *Pioneer 10* spacecraft
1970	Drake becomes director of National Astronomy and Ionosphere Center
1972	*Pioneer 10* launched on March 2
1973	*Pioneer 11* launched on April 5
1974	On November 16, Arecibo Observatory sends first radio signal deliberately transmitted to extraterrestrial civilizations
1975	Drake steps down as associate director of Center for Radiophysics and Space Research
1976	Drake becomes Goldwin Smith Professor of Astronomy at Cornell
1977	*Voyager 1* and *Voyager 2* spacecraft launched, carrying phonograph records of voices, sounds, and images from Earth
1978	On February 16, Senator William Proxmire gives a NASA SETI proposal a Golden Fleece Award, suggesting that such projects are a waste of money
1981	Drake steps down as director of National Astronomy and Ionosphere Center
1982	Proxmire obtains passage of a congressional amendment blocking funding for SETI projects; Carl Sagan persuades Proxmire to drop his opposition to SETI; committee of the National Academy of Sciences recommends that SETI be established as a national goal; *Science* publishes letter in support of SETI composed by Carl Sagan and signed by 72 other scientists, including seven Nobel Prize winners, in its October 29 issue
1983	Congress restores limited funding for NASA SETI projects
1984	Drake joins University of California, Santa Cruz, and founds SETI Institute in Mountain View, California

1988	NASA begins work on major SETI project
1993	On September 22, Congress cancels funding for NASA SETI project
1994	Supporters obtain private funding for project
1995	In February, Project Phoenix begins observations; astronomers find first evidence of planets circling other stars
1996	Drake retires from University of California, Santa Cruz
1999	University of California, Berkeley, releases SETI@home software in May; in October, Drake gives Jansky Lecture
2004	Project Phoenix ends in March

Further Reading

Books

Drake, Frank, and Dava Sobel. *Is Anyone Out There? The Scientific Search for Extraterrestrial Intelligence.* New York: Dell, 1992.
> Memoir of Drake's life and experiences with SETI up to the time of the NASA project that became Project Phoenix.

Ward, Peter D., and Donald Brownlee. *Rare Earth: Why Complex Life Is Uncommon in the Universe.* New York: Springer Verlag Telos, 2000.
> A paleontologist and an astronomer offer reasons for believing that complex, intelligent life is rare in the universe, perhaps unique to Earth.

Articles

Crease, Robert P., and Charles C. Mann. "The Search for Life on Other Planets." *Atlantic* 254 (November 1984): 122–127.
> Describes SETI research up to the beginning of the NASA SETI project, including Frank Drake's role.

Drake, Frank D. "A Reminiscence of Project Ozma." *Cosmic Search* 1, no. 1 (January 1979). Available online. URL: http://www.bigear.org/vol1no1/ozma.htm. Accessed on September 26, 2005.
> Drake's personal account of the first search for communication from intelligent extraterrestrial life, which he conducted in April and May

1960 at the National Radio Astronomy Observatory in Green Bank, West Virginia.

Gorman, Jessica. "How to Eavesdrop at a Cosmological Waterhole." University of California, Santa Cruz, Science Notes, 1997. Available online. URL: http://scicom.ucsc.edu/SciNotes/9701/full/features/seti/SETIstory2.html. Accessed on January 29, 2005.
Describes SETI research in 1997, with frequent quotes from Frank Drake.

Morrison, Philip, and Giuseppe Cocconi. "Searching for Interstellar Communications." *Nature* 184 (September 19, 1959): 844–846.
Early scientific paper recommending use of radio telescopes to search for signals sent by civilizations on planets circling nearby stars.

Owen, Robert M. "A Brief SETI Chronology." SETI League. Available online. URL: http://www.setileague.org/general/history.htm. Accessed on March 9, 2005.
Chronological listing of major SETI projects and other events important in SETI history, from 1959 to 1999.

Sagan, Carl, Linda Salzman Sagan, and Frank Drake. "A Message from Earth." *Science* 175 (February 25, 1972): 881–884.
Scientific article describes the design of the aluminum message plate placed aboard the *Pioneer 10* spacecraft and explains why each feature of the design was chosen.

Squeri, Lawrence. "When ET Calls, SETI Is Ready." *Journal of Popular Culture* 37 (February 2004): 478–497.
Long, meaty article recounts the history of SETI and people's reactions to it.

Web Sites

SETI@home. Available online. URL: http://setiathome.berkeley.edu. Accessed on September 26, 2005.
SETI@home is a scientific experiment that uses Internet-connected computers to participate in the Search for Extraterrestrial Intelligence (SETI). Screen-saver software, available on the site for free downloading, allows users' computers to analyze radio telescope data for possible extraterrestrial signals when the computers are not in use. The site explains the software and its use and provides statistics, profiles of users, technical news, and other information about the project.

SETI Institute. Available online. URL: http://www.seti.org. Accessed on September 26, 2005.

This privately funded institute, founded by Frank Drake in 1984 and located in Mountain View, California, pursues a number of projects dedicated to the Search for Extraterrestrial Intelligence and related goals. The institute's Web site provides information about these projects and the institute as a whole, as well as news stories related to SETI.

X-RAY SUPERMAN

RICCARDO GIACCONI AND X-RAY ASTRONOMY

When German physicist Wilhelm Röntgen discovered X-rays in 1895, he found that this mysterious radiation could pass through materials that block light, creating images that human eyes had never seen before. Within a few days of his discovery, for example, he used the rays to make a ghostly photograph showing the bones of his wife's hand.

X-rays penetrate dark clouds of gas in interstellar space as easily as they passed through the flesh of Bertha Röntgen's fingers. Because of this, telescopes that detect X-rays produced images as new and strange to astronomers of the late 20th century as X-ray images of the body seemed to early 20th-century physicians. The inventor of X-ray telescopes, and the driving force in making such telescopes valued tools in astronomy, is Italian-born astrophysicist Riccardo Giacconi.

Riccardo Giacconi invented the X-ray telescope and worked tirelessly to persuade NASA to launch satellites that would give astronomers "X-ray vision." He won a share of the Nobel Prize in physics in 2002. (Johns Hopkins University)

Tracking Rays from Space

Riccardo Giacconi's mother, Elsa Canni Giacconi, taught high school mathematics and physics, but Riccardo himself did not care for school. He was often in trouble, sometimes for skipping class, sometimes for pointing out his teachers' mistakes. Born on October 6, 1931, in Genoa, Giacconi grew up in Milan. His parents separated when he was very young, and his mother and stepfather, Antonio Giacconi, raised him.

In spite of his poor attitude in class, Giacconi's grades on tests were good enough to let him skip his senior year of high school and begin attending the University of Milan in 1950. He majored in physics, earning his Ph.D. in that subject in 1954. He specialized in the study of cosmic rays, which are protons and other high-energy subatomic particles that come from space. Before "atom-smasher" machines were developed in the late 1950s, physicists learned about the behavior of subatomic particles mainly by observing cosmic rays and the rays' interactions with Earth's atmosphere.

Giacconi remained at Milan as an assistant physics professor for two years after he earned his doctorate. In 1956, however, he obtained a Fulbright Fellowship to continue cosmic ray research at the University of Indiana, Bloomington. While there, he married Mirella Manaira, an Italian woman he had known since high school. He did further postdoctoral work at Princeton University's cosmic ray laboratory in 1958–59.

At about this time, a coworker on one of Giacconi's projects introduced him to the president of American Science and Engineering, Inc. (AS&E), a small private research firm in Cambridge, Massachusetts. Hoping to obtain contracts from the newly established National Aeronautics and Space Administration (NASA), the company's managers asked Giacconi to develop a space research program for them. Giacconi was tired of the slow pace of cosmic-ray research and wanted a new challenge, so he accepted. He become AS&E's head of space sciences in September 1959.

A New Kind of Telescope

Soon after Giacconi's arrival at AS&E, a conversation at a party gave him an idea about what kind of program to develop. Bruno

Rossi, chairman of the board of AS&E and the party's host, suggested that Giacconi investigate X-ray astronomy. The Space Science Board of the National Academy of Sciences had recently concluded that the field had some potential, Rossi said.

Giacconi found little to investigate. Radio astronomy was beginning to join optical astronomy as a respectable field of research, but X-ray astronomy seemed unlikely to follow because the Earth's atmosphere blocks out X-rays and other forms of high-energy electromagnetic radiation. X-rays from space could be recorded only when detectors were lifted at least 100 miles (161 km) above the planet's surface in rockets or balloons. Such detectors operated for just a few minutes before crashing back to Earth.

Only one group of astronomers had made much use of X-rays, Giacconi learned. In September 1949, Herbert Friedman and others at the Naval Research Laboratory in Washington, D.C., had sent up a captured German V-2 rocket carrying Geiger counters modified to pick up X-rays. The counters spotted such rays coming from the Sun's corona, the shell of hot gas above the star's atmosphere. The Sun's X-radiation was just 1 millionth as strong as its light, however, so most astronomers thought that X-rays from any other star would be undetectable.

Nonetheless, Giacconi was intrigued by Rossi's suggestion. X-rays might be more useful to astronomers, he thought, if an actual telescope, rather than just a counter, could be made to receive them. Giacconi knew that an X-ray telescope would look nothing like an optical telescope because X-rays pass right through ordinary telescope mirrors. X-rays could be focused by a reflecting mirror, however, if they hit the mirror by sliding along the mirror's surface, like a bullet grazing off a wall.

In the 1940s and 1950s, Hans Wolter, a German physicist, had shown that X-ray images could be made with a combination of two mirrors, one with a paraboloid shape and the other with a hyperboloid shape. The mirrors had to be aligned nearly parallel to the incoming rays. X-rays grazed along one mirror, bounced to the other, and were then focused. Wolter had tried to make X-ray microscopes and failed, but Giacconi thought that making the larger mirrors used by telescopes would be easier.

A mirror that could focus X-rays, Giacconi realized, would be shaped more or less like a cylinder, such as a tin can or a drinking glass. Bruno Rossi suggested that several mirrors could be nested one inside the other to increase the total area available for collecting the rays. By 1960, Giacconi and Rossi had designed an X-ray telescope and described it in a scientific paper. Giacconi also became a naturalized U.S. citizen in that year.

X-Ray Star

Giacconi did not have the technology to make or the opportunity to fly his new telescopes for several years. Meanwhile, however, he persuaded the managers of an air force research program to let him send up detectors on a rocket to look for solar X-rays reflected from the Moon. His experiment was launched from White Sands Missile Range, in southern New Mexico, on June 18, 1962.

The detectors found no X-rays coming from the Moon during the 350 seconds they had for scanning the sky. However, they made two far more startling discoveries. First, they showed that the entire sky was washed in a low level of X-radiation. This radiation was so even and widespread that it had to come from outside the Milky Way galaxy. The second discovery was an intense beam of X-rays pouring out of a spot in the constellation Scorpio (the scorpion). The unknown object producing the rays, which Giacconi called Sco X-1, was the first astronomical X-ray source other than the Sun to be located.

Sco X-1 was "a truly amazing and new type of celestial object," Giacconi recalled in his 2002 Nobel Prize lecture. Herbert Friedman confirmed the object's existence in April 1963. In 1966, Giacconi and other scientists found a faint star in the spot where the X-rays originated. The star appeared dim because it was very far away, but it proved to be actually a thousand times brighter than the Sun. Its X-ray intensity, in turn, was a thousand times as great as that of its visible light. At the time, no one knew how a star could generate so much energy.

The results of his 1962 flight convinced Giacconi that X-ray maps of space could be very valuable in astronomy. They could reveal places where explosions or other events had released tremendous amounts of energy. On September 25, 1963, he and Herbert Gursky, another AS&E scientist, proposed a program of X-ray astronomy research to NASA, ending with the launching of a four-foot (1.2-m) diameter X-ray telescope into Earth's orbit. Giacconi thought the program could be completed by the end of the 1960s. He was wrong by about 30 years.

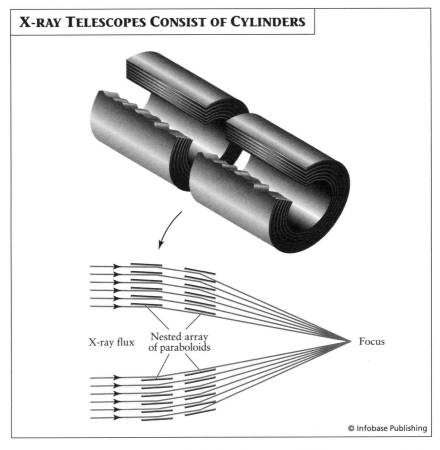

X-RAY TELESCOPES CONSIST OF CYLINDERS

X-ray flux   Nested array of paraboloids   Focus

© Infobase Publishing

X-ray telescopes consist of nested cylinders, like cans of different sizes stacked inside one another. The first group of mirrors in the cylinders are paraboloid in shape, and a second set has a shape called hyperboloid. X-rays graze off these mirrors and are focused at the end of the telescope.

Uhuru

Giacconi went on working at AS&E during the 1960s, becoming executive vice president of the company by 1969. He sent an X-ray telescope into space for the first time in October 1963 and also helped to develop the X-ray telescope flown aboard NASA's Skylab mission in 1968. Most of his and other X-ray astronomers' work in this decade focused on the Sun, although they discovered hundreds of other X-ray sources as well.

All X-ray astronomy experiments in the 1960s were made on rocket and balloon flights, and Giacconi calculated that, put together, they amounted to a mere hour of observation time. The field would really advance, he felt, only when X-ray detectors could remain aloft for years in a satellite. After a decade of arguing with other astronomers and NASA officials, he finally got his wish on December 12, 1970, when the world's first X-ray observatory satellite was launched from the East African country of Kenya. Giacconi honored the date, the anniversary of Kenya's independence, by naming the satellite *Uhuru,* the Swahili word for "freedom."

Uhuru remained in service a little over two years, finally crashing back into the atmosphere and burning up in March 1973. During that time, it brought astronomers the first glimpses of a new universe whose beauty and violence no one could have imagined. Wallace and Karen Tucker write in *The Cosmic Inquirers,* their book about modern telescopes and their makers, that Giacconi called interpreting *Uhuru*'s data "the scientific highlight of my career. It was the most mystical moment, when we suddenly understood."

Unequal Partners

For the first time, thanks to *Uhuru,* astronomers could study single X-ray sources for long periods to see how the sources' pattern of radiation changed over time. Giacconi and others found that some stars gave off X-rays in pulses, like a light flashing on and off. The intensity of the stars' X-ray beams also varied, either in a regular pattern or in a seemingly random way. Sometimes the stars stopped sending X-ray signals entirely for several days, then started up again.

I Was There: The Launch of *Uhuru*

After several delays, the launch of the *Uhuru* satellite was scheduled for sunrise on December 12, 1970. The satellite was to be sent up from a converted oil drilling platform off the coast of Kenya. Like an anxious parent hovering over a sick child, Riccardo Giacconi spent the night before the launch on the platform, which belonged to an Italian company. Giacconi told Wallace and Karen Tucker, "It was wet and cold out there, and I began to get chilled. I couldn't sleep. One of the Italian crew members literally gave me the shirt off his back, so I could get a few minutes' sleep and be ready for the launch."

Dawn came and went, but problems continued to hold up the launch. As the Sun rose higher in the sky, the temperature on the platform rose as well. Giacconi was afraid that heat and humidity would damage the delicate detectors in the spacecraft, but he was equally determined that the satellite should go up that day.

Finally, the Tuckers report, a rocket lifted *Uhuru* into orbit a little after noon. Then came Giacconi's next anxious question: Were the detectors working? He recounted to the Tuckers,

I had to know. I couldn't wait until [the] Goddard [Space Flight Center in Greenbelt, Maryland] decided to turn on the instruments. I convinced Marjory Townsend [the NASA manager for the Uhuru project, who was with him in Kenya] to break with protocol and take a peek when the satellite made its first passage over Kenya, about an hour and a half later. We jumped in one of those rubber boats and rushed back to camp, some 3 miles away. We reached the control van just in time to turn on the high voltage to the detectors, just to see if they were working. They were, perfectly, so we shut them off again. We were like kids, we were so excited.

Combining data from *Uhuru* and optical telescopes, Giacconi and other scientists eventually concluded that many X-ray stars, including Giacconi's original find, Sco X-1, were really two stars in one. They were so-called binary systems, in which a pair of stars circle around one another in a close orbit. In most cases, the astronomers decided, one star was a normal type and the other was a tiny, strange object called a neutron star.

A neutron star is produced when a star about 10 times larger than the Sun ends its life in a gigantic explosion termed a *supernova*. The explosion throws most of the mass of the star into space, leaving behind a highly magnetized, rapidly spinning core that is only about 12 miles (20 km) across, yet contains as much mass as the Sun. A neutron star is so dense that most of the electrons and protons within it are squashed together to form neutrons. A piece of neutron star the size of a sugar cube would weigh a billion tons (0.907 billion metric tons).

In binary systems containing a neutron star, the intense gravity and strong magnetic field of the neutron star peel a stream of gas from the atmosphere of its larger companion. As the gas swirls around the neutron star, forming a disk, and then spirals down onto the star's surface, the gas's movement accelerates to nearly the speed of light. This acceleration heats the gas so much that it sends out high-energy X-rays. The X-ray signal disappears temporarily when the normal star passes in front of the neutron star, blocking the stream of rays from astronomers' detectors.

The First Black Holes

When X-ray signals from a binary star system did not follow a regular pattern, Giacconi and other astrophysicists concluded that the gas from the large companion star was being pulled into something even more bizarre than a neutron star: a black hole. Theorists had predicted the possibility of black holes since the 1930s, but many astronomers had doubted whether these objects actually existed, or at least whether they could ever be observed. In 1974, however, Giacconi and others showed that the *Uhuru* data for an X-ray source called Cygnus X-1 (the first such source discovered in the constellation of Cygnus, the swan) presented the first solid evidence of a black hole.

Star-size black holes are thought to be created when giant stars, with more than 10 times the mass of the Sun, use up all their nuclear fuel and collapse in on themselves. These stars, like the smaller ones that make neutron stars, throw off most of their mass in a supernova explosion. Instead of creating a neutron star from what is left, however, they produce an object even more dense—not much bigger than a neutron star but at least three times as massive. The gravity of a black hole is so powerful that it bends, or warps, space itself. The warp acts like a whirlpool, pulling all matter and energy from the surrounding area into the black hole. Nothing, not even light, can escape. As with the binary pairs containing neutron stars, the black holes in binary pairs like Cygnus X-1 pull gas from their normal companions. As the gas circles around the black hole before disappearing into it, the gas moves so fast and becomes so hot that it gives off X-rays.

The discovery of binary star systems that sent out X-rays greatly increased the available information on neutron stars and black holes. It showed a new way for celestial objects to generate energy,

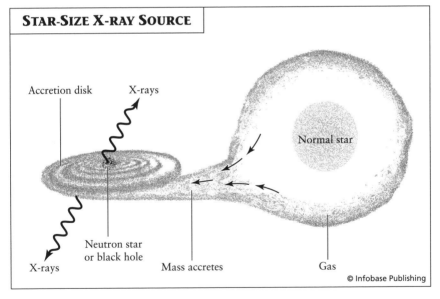

Many star-size X-ray sources appear to be pairs of unequal stars that orbit one another in a binary system. One member of the pair is a very small, very dense neutron star or an even denser black hole. The intense gravity of the neutron star or black hole pulls a stream of gas from the surface of its companion, a normal star. As the gas circles around the neutron star or black hole, it speeds up and becomes very hot. As a result, it gives off high-energy X-rays.

by pulling gas and other material into a strong gravitational field. Such activity could produce 50 times more energy than an atomic fusion reaction, Giacconi explained in his 2002 Nobel Prize lecture. The supermassive black holes now thought to lie at the centers of quasars and some, perhaps most, galaxies are believed to generate unbelievable amounts of energy by the same process, applied on a tremendously larger scale.

Uhuru also showed powerful X-rays streaming from clusters of galaxies. Giacconi and other researchers concluded that the rays come from invisible, extremely hot gas filling the space between the galaxies in the clusters. They calculated that the gas had to have as much mass as all the visible matter in the galaxies combined. In effect, they said, the universe contained twice as much matter as anyone had thought—but half of it could not be seen with optical telescopes. Only the "X-ray vision" of the detectors that Giacconi had helped to design revealed it.

Einstein

In 1970, even before the launch of *Uhuru,* NASA agreed to fund four large High-Energy Astronomy Observatory (HEAO) satellites during the coming decade. Instead of mere detectors like those on *Uhuru,* the third HEAO satellite was scheduled to contain a four-foot (1.2-m) X-ray telescope. Riccardo Giacconi greatly looked forward to seeing his 1960 invention produce images of distant stars for the first time. Early in 1973, however, he was devastated to learn that the space agency, trying to save money because the Mars Viking lander program was costing more than expected, had canceled the HEAO project on January 2.

Giacconi, along with other scientists working on the HEAO satellites and several NASA officials who supported the program, begged the agency's management to reconsider. They eventually succeeded—partly. NASA reestablished the HEAO program in July 1974 but with only half the funding that the program had originally been given. This meant that many of the scientists had to scale back or even abandon their projects. Giacconi, for instance, was forced to settle for a telescope only half the size of the one he had planned.

The scaled-down X-ray observatory satellite was launched on November 13, 1978. Giacconi and the satellite's other developers named it *Einstein* to honor the centennial of the great physicist-mathematician's birth. The *Einstein* satellite carried an X-ray telescope consisting of four nested pairs of nearly cylindrical mirrors, each about two feet (0.6 m) across, as well as four types of detectors. It remained in operation until April 26, 1981.

Among other things, data from *Einstein* finally solved the mystery of the cosmic background X-radiation, whose origin had been a puzzle since Giacconi discovered the radiation in 1962. Unlike the background radio radiation that Arno Penzias and Robert Wilson had identified in 1964, the X-radiation appeared to come from particular sources in space, chiefly quasars.

Hard-Driving Manager

Giacconi oversaw the Einstein project from an office at the Harvard-Smithsonian Center for Astrophysics in Cambridge, Massachusetts. He had become associate director of the center's high-energy physics division, as well as a full professor of astronomy at Harvard, in 1973. While he was looking over the new satellite's data, NASA was planning the biggest satellite observatory of all—what would later be called the *Hubble Space Telescope.*

In 1981, the space agency established a new organization, the Space Telescope Science Institute (STScI), to control the scientific part of the Hubble project. The institute was set up on the Homewood campus of Johns Hopkins University in Baltimore. NASA asked Giacconi to become STScI's first director, and he accepted. When he took up that post in September 1981, he also became a professor of astronomy at Johns Hopkins.

In his years at STScI, Giacconi perfected the hard-driving style of management that he had developed at AS&E and honed while controlling large scientific projects and battling NASA. (A Johns Hopkins University press release, issued when Giacconi won the Nobel Prize in physics in 2002, quoted Hopkins astronomy professor Timothy Heckman as saying that Giacconi "could've been, say, president of General Motors if he hadn't been drawn into astrophysics.") The

Italian scientist did his best to make the telescope institute a world-class scientific center and to improve the planning of the Hubble project, which he called "a disaster" in his Nobel autobiography. For instance, as he had done with *Uhuru* and *Einstein,* he upgraded the computer software and procedures that would manage and analyze data coming from the telescope.

"Nothing is going to happen unless you work with your life's blood," Giacconi told Ann K. Finkbeiner, the author of an article about him published in *The Sciences* in 1993, just after he ended his term as the director of STScI. His energy and impatience became even more legendary during his years at the telescope institute than they had been before. As a result, he was not always popular. Even those who did not agree with him, however, usually respected him. That respect was reflected in the numerous awards that Giacconi won during the 1980s, including the Astronomical Society of the Pacific's Bruce Medal (1981), the Dannie Heineman Prize from the American Institute of Physics (1981), the Gold Medal of Britain's Royal Astronomical Society (1982), and a share of the prestigious Wolf Prize in physics (1987).

In January 1993, Giacconi gave up his directorship of STScI and moved to Munich, Germany, to become director general of the European Southern Observatory (ESO). He made the move partly to escape painful memories of his son's death in a car crash, as well as his own continued frustration with NASA. At ESO, Giacconi helped to set up the Very Large Telescope (VLT), an array of four 26.4-foot (8-m) optical telescopes (plus several smaller telescopes) in Chile. At the time, the VLT was the largest ground-based astronomy program ever undertaken. In 1998, the year the first stage of the VLT was completed, he also helped to establish a cooperative program between the United States, Canada, and ESO to build the Atacama Large Millimeter Array (ALMA), a second astronomical installation in Chile (in the Atacama Desert). He took charge of the North American part of the ALMA project in 1999.

Chandra

Giacconi's term as ESO director ended in June 1999, and he returned to the United States in July. He rejoined Johns Hopkins as a research professor. He also became president of Associated Universities, Inc., the organization that comanages the National Radio Astronomy Observatory (NRAO) with the National Science Foundation. He kept this position until 2004.

Giacconi arrived just in time for a bittersweet celebration—seeing a longtime dream come true, but not under his management. Throughout his years with NASA, he had pushed for the launch of a 3.9-foot (1.2-m) X-ray telescope, but without success. When he moved on to other projects, Harvey Tananbaum, his coauthor on a proposal for the telescope written in 1976, continued the effort from the Harvard-Smithsonian Center for Astrophysics. The telescope was finally sent into space on July 23, 1999, just a few weeks after Giacconi came back to the United States. It was called the *Chandra X-ray Observatory* to honor Indian-born astrophysicist Subrahmanyan Chandrasekhar, who had done important work on

The Chandra X-ray Observatory, *launched in 1999 and named after astrophysicist Subrahmanyan Chandrasekhar, was the fulfillment of a longtime dream for Riccardo Giacconi. Giacconi had pressured NASA to launch a large X-ray telescope satellite since the early 1970s. (NASA/CXC/NGST)*

the structure and evolution of stars. Some people said, however, that it could just as well have been named after Giacconi.

Not surprisingly, Giacconi was eager to use the new observatory. In the early 2000s, he was the principal investigator for the *Chandra* ultra-deep survey, which has provided X-ray images of very distant objects, reaching far back in time to the early days of the universe. In March 2001, for instance, the *Chandra* Deep-Field South image, a 261-hour-long exposure that is one of the most sensitive X-ray images ever made, revealed that supermassive black holes had been much more common in the young universe than they are today.

Giacconi also used *Chandra* to make further progress in identifying sources of the cosmic background X-radiation. He matched faint X-ray sources in *Chandra* images with equally faint galaxies and quasars photographed optically with the *Hubble Space Telescope* and the Very Large Telescope. In this way, he combined the power of several different instruments that owed part of their existence to him.

The early 2000s brought even more honors to Giacconi. The most important was a share of the Nobel Prize in physics, which he won in 2002. He was also awarded the Karl Schwartzschild Medal from the German Astronomical Society in 2004 and the U.S. National Medal of Science (for 2003) in March 2005. In 2004, he rose to the highest rank at Johns Hopkins, that of university professor.

Today detectors aboard satellites such as *Chandra* let astronomers see all the shades of the "invisible rainbow" of electromagnetic radiation, from gamma rays—the most energetic type of radiation—to radio waves. Data from these orbiting observatories, especially those that pick up X-rays or other high-energy radiation, have changed astronomers' understanding of the cosmos. "Gone is the classic conception of the Universe as . . . serene and majestic," Riccardo Giacconi said in his 2002 Nobel lecture. "The Universe we know today is pervaded by the echoes of enormous explosions. . . . From the initial explosion to formation of galaxies and clusters, from the birth to the death of stars, high energy phenomena are the norm." This new picture owes its existence to pioneers such as Giacconi, who first let astronomers, like the comic-book hero Superman, see the universe with X-ray vision.

Chronology

1895	Wilhelm Röntgen discovers X-rays
1931	Riccardo Giacconi born in Genoa, Italy, on October 6
1949	Herbert Friedman detects X-rays from the Sun's corona in September
1950s	Friedman continues solar X-ray research; Hans Wolter shows how mirrors can capture X-rays
1950	Giacconi begins attending University of Milan
1954	Giacconi earns Ph.D. in cosmic-ray physics
1954–56	Giacconi remains in Milan as assistant physics professor
1956–58	Giacconi does cosmic-ray research on a Fulbright fellowship at University of Indiana, Bloomington; he marries Mirella Manaira
1958–59	Giacconi does further postdoctoral research at Princeton University cosmic-ray laboratory
1959	Giacconi becomes head of space sciences at American Science and Engineering (AS&E) in September; Bruno Rossi of AS&E suggests that Giacconi investigate X-ray astronomy
1960	Giacconi and Rossi design an X-ray telescope; Giacconi becomes a naturalized U.S. citizen
1962	X-ray detectors launched with rocket on June 18 discover cosmic background X-radiation and first extrasolar X-ray source, Sco X-1
1963	Herbert Friedman confirms existence of Sco X-1 in April; Giacconi and Herbert Gursky propose program of X-ray astronomy research to NASA on September 25; first X-ray telescope sent into space in October
1966	Giacconi and others find a faint star in the location of Sco X-1
1968	Skylab mission includes an X-ray telescope designed by Giacconi

1969	Giacconi becomes executive vice president of AS&E
1970	NASA agrees to fund four High-Energy Astronomy Observatory (HEAO) satellites, including one carrying an X-ray telescope; *Uhuru*, first X-ray astronomy satellite, launched on December 12
1970–75	Using data from *Uhuru*, Giacconi and other astronomers show that Sco X-1 and many other X-ray sources consist of a normal star paired with a neutron star; *Uhuru* data provide the first convincing proof of the existence of black holes; *Uhuru* reveals hidden gas clouds within clusters of galaxies, doubling the amount of known matter in the universe
1973	NASA cancels HEAO program on January 2; *Uhuru* falls back to Earth in March; Giacconi becomes associate director of high-energy physics division at the Harvard-Smithsonian Center for Astrophysics and full professor of astronomy at Harvard
1974	In July, NASA reinstates HEAO program with half its original funding
1976	Giacconi and Harvey Tananbaum coauthor a proposal for a satellite carrying a 3.9-foot (1.2-m) X-ray telescope
1978	*Einstein* X-ray telescope satellite launched on November 13
1978–81	*Einstein* data show that most, if not all, cosmic background X-radiation comes from quasars and other specific sources
1981	*Einstein* falls back to Earth on April 26; In September, Giacconi becomes first director of Space Telescope Science Institute and professor of astronomy at Johns Hopkins University
1982	Giacconi wins Gold Medal of the Royal Astronomical Society
1987	Giacconi wins share of Wolf Prize in physics
1993	Giacconi steps down from directorship of Space Telescope Science Institute in January and becomes director general of European Southern Observatory (ESO) in Munich, Germany

1995–99	Giacconi oversees Very Large Telescope project and helps to set up Atacama Large Millimeter Array
1999	Giacconi ends term as director of ESO in June and returns to United States in July; *Chandra X-ray Observatory* satellite launched on July 23; Giacconi becomes president of Associated Universities, Inc., and head of North American part of ALMA project; he also becomes research professor at Johns Hopkins
2001	In March, Giacconi manages project that produces *Chandra* Deep-Field South image, showing supermassive black holes in the early universe
2002	On October 8, Giacconi awarded a share of the Nobel Prize in physics
2004	Giacconi receives Karl Schwartzschild Medal from German Astronomical Society and becomes university professor at Johns Hopkins
2005	In March, Giacconi receives National Medal of Science

Further Reading

Books

Tucker, Wallace, and Karen Tucker. *The Cosmic Inquirers: Modern Telescopes and Their Makers.* Cambridge, Mass.: Harvard University Press, 1986.
> Contains a long chapter on Giacconi and the development of the *Einstein* satellite.

Articles

Finkbeiner, Ann K. "X-ray Impresario." *The Sciences* 33 (May–June 1993): 10–13.
> Vivid portrayal of Giacconi's intense personality and aggressive management style as head of the Space Telescope Science Institute, including confrontations with NASA. Also describes his scientific achievements in X-ray astronomy.

Giacconi, Riccardo, and Bruno Rossi. "A 'Telescope' for Soft X-ray Astronomy." *Journal of Geophysical Research* 65 (1960): 773.

> Paper in which Giacconi describes a method for building an X-ray telescope.

———— et al. "Evidence for X-rays from Sources outside the Solar System." *Physical Review Letters* 9 (December 1, 1962): 439.

> Paper in which Giacconi's team reports on their rocket flight with X-ray detectors on June 18, 1962, which produced the first evidence of cosmic X-ray sources other than the Sun.

Johns Hopkins University. "Physics Nobel Prize Winner Holds Hopkins Research Position." Available online. URL: http://www.jhu.edu/news_info/news/home02/oct02/nobel.html. Posted on October 8, 2002. Accessed on January 29, 2005.

> Brief press release issued when Giacconi won the Nobel Prize in physics.

Nobelprize.org. "The Dawn of X-ray Astronomy." Riccardo Giacconi's Nobel lecture, presented December 8, 2002. Available online. URL: http://nobelprize.org/physics/laureates/2002/giacconi-lecture.html. Accessed on September 26, 2005.

> Lengthy, rather technical description of the development of X-ray astronomy and important discoveries in the field.

————. "Riccardo Giacconi—Autobiography." Excerpted from *Les Prix Nobel 2002*. Available online. URL: http://nobelprize.org/physics/laureates/2002/giacconi-autobio.html. Accessed on January 29, 2005.

> Autobiographical sketch written after Giacconi won a share of the Nobel Prize in physics in 2002.

Tucker, Wallace H. "The X-ray Universe." *Beam Line,* summer 1995. Available online. URL: http://www.slac.stanford.edu/pubs/beamline/25/2/25-2-tucker.pdf. Accessed on September 26, 2005.

> Clear, well-illustrated description of major discoveries in X-ray astronomy to 1995.

Waldrop, M. Mitchell. "Space Telescope (II): A Science Institute." *Science* 22 (August 5, 1983): 534–536.

> Describes the founding of the Space Telescope Science Institute and its early days under Giacconi's directorship.

Web Site

The *Chandra* Chronicles. Available online. URL: http://chandra.
harvard.edu/chronicle. The main *Chandra* site is at http://chandra.
harvard.edu. Accessed on March 19, 2005.
Produced by the Harvard-Smithsonian Center for Astrophysics, which
manages the *Chandra X-ray Observatory,* this site contains descriptions of major milestones in X-ray astronomy, various X-ray observatory satellites, how X-ray telescopes differ from optical telescopes,
and more. It also includes links to educational materials, images, press
releases, and other resources.

7

AN EYE IN SPACE

LYMAN SPITZER, JR., AND THE
HUBBLE SPACE TELESCOPE

Twinkle, twinkle, little star!
How I wonder what you are.

This rhyme may charm children, but to astronomers, "twinkling" is just one of the dirty tricks that Earth's atmosphere plays to keep them from learning what stars are. Swirling currents of air and dust distort light coming from space, making stars and planets seem to shimmer when seen from the ground. In many places, air pollution and the glow of electric lights from nearby cities dim these heavenly objects as well. As a result, even the best optical telescopes on Earth often appear to be very dirty glasses. Furthermore, except for scientists working with radio waves, astronomers who want to examine radiation above and below the wavelengths of visible light are even worse off than optical astronomers if they stay on the ground. They are essentially blind because the planet's thick blanket of air blocks out this radiation almost entirely.

To Lyman Spitzer, Jr., the answer to these problems was obvious: Put telescopes in space, high above the annoying atmosphere. When he first suggested this idea in 1946, however, his solution was far from obvious to anyone else. No one had yet sent a rocket high enough to go into orbit around the Earth, let alone placed any objects there. Most astronomers thought that, even if a telescope could someday be put into orbit, it could not be controlled well enough to make it useful to science. Nonetheless, Spitzer neither gave up his vision nor his attempts to persuade scientists and politicians to make it a reality. The *Hubble Space Telescope,* launched in 1990, owes its existence largely to him.

From Sonar to Stars

Born on June 26, 1914, Lyman Spitzer grew up in Toledo, Ohio. Spitzer wrote in *Dreams, Stars, and Electrons,* a book of memoirs and reprinted papers from his long and distinguished scientific career, that an inspiring teacher at Phillips Academy, a prestigious boarding school in Andover, Massachusetts, stirred his interest in physics and astronomy during his teenage years. Temporarily putting astronomy aside, Spitzer majored in physics as an undergraduate at Yale University, from which he earned his bachelor's degree in 1935.

Lyman Spitzer, Jr., pointed out the advantages of placing a telescope in space in 1946, more than 10 years before satellites of any kind were launched. Spitzer did more than perhaps any other person to make the Hubble Space Telescope *a reality. (Trustees of Princeton University)*

As a graduate student, Spitzer combined his two interests by studying astrophysics, first at Britain's Cambridge University and then at Princeton University in New Jersey. He obtained a master's degree from Princeton in 1937 and a Ph.D. in 1938—the first Ph.D. in theoretical astrophysics that the university had ever awarded. He did a year of postdoctoral research at Harvard, then joined the Yale faculty in 1939.

The United States' entry into World War II in December 1941 interrupted Spitzer's career. From early 1942 to 1946, the young scientist worked in New York City and later in Washington, D.C., for the National Defense Research Committee. He helped to develop sonar, the technique of determining the size and position of submarines or other objects by sending sound waves into water and analyzing the echoes that the objects reflect. "We sank submarines on the 64th floor of the Empire State Building," Spitzer told Wallace and Karen Tucker, as they report in *Modern Telescopes and Their Makers*.

Spitzer returned briefly to Yale after the war, then moved to Princeton in 1947. Even though he was only 33 years old, the university made him head of its astrophysics department and director of its observatory, posts he held until 1979. Spitzer became the Charles A. Young Professor of Astronomy in 1952 and remained at Princeton until 1982, when he reached the university's mandatory retirement age of 68.

Pioneering Research

During his long and prolific career, Lyman Spitzer focused on three subjects besides development of a space telescope: the study of the gas and dust between stars; the evolution of stars, star clusters, and galaxies; and the physics of plasma, a superhot, electrically charged, gaslike form of matter in which electrons move freely rather than being attached to atomic nuclei. He did pioneering work in all these fields.

Spitzer essentially founded the study of interstellar gas and dust. He studied the chemical composition and temperature of dust grains in deep space and showed how they interact with magnetic fields. He showed how gas is distributed in space and correctly predicted the existence of a halo of hot gas around the Milky Way.

Spitzer's studies of interstellar gas led to other research showing how stars, star clusters, and galaxies change over time. He concluded that young, very bright stars called supergiants have formed relatively recently, and are still forming, from this gas, an idea confirmed by evidence discovered in the 1960s and later. He proposed that collisions with large gas clouds speed up the movement of stars in star clusters, causing some of the outer stars to escape from the clusters' gravitational field. As a result, the clusters shrink and become more dense with age and eventually collapse. Spitzer later suggested that collisions between galaxies cause the centers of the galaxies to evolve in much the same way as star clusters.

Spitzer believed that the fusion of atomic nuclei in plasma, which occurs in the Sun and other stars, could someday be harnessed to provide a nonpolluting form of energy. Before this could be done, a way had to be developed to hold the plasma together because the matching charges on the protons in the plasma make the particles repel each other. Spitzer designed a possible device for confining a plasma, which he called the Stellarator, in early 1951. Later that same year, he persuaded the U.S. Atomic Energy Commission to fund a research project on controlled thermonuclear fusion at Princeton. When this program, originally called Project Matterhorn, was renamed the Princeton Plasma Physics Laboratory in 1958, Spitzer was made the laboratory's director. He kept this position until 1967.

Impossible Dream?

Important as Lyman Spitzer's other achievements were to fellow scientists, the world is most likely to remember him as the "father" of the *Hubble Space Telescope*. Spitzer first suggested the idea of a space telescope in a memorandum to RAND, a research organization sponsored by the U.S. Air Force, in 1946. The air force was thinking of trying to put a satellite into orbit around the Earth, and RAND officials wanted to know what scientific uses such a satellite might have.

Spitzer's report, titled "Astronomical Advantages of an Extraterrestrial Observatory," is reprinted in *Dreams, Stars, and Electrons*. In it, Spitzer suggested that a satellite carrying a small spectroscope might record ultraviolet radiation from space, which could not be detected on Earth except in the highest atmosphere. This device could provide new information about the Sun and its effect on the electrically charged layer of the Earth's upper atmosphere, the ionosphere. Adding a small optical telescope to the satellite would increase its usefulness still further.

Best of all, Spitzer thought, would be to send a large reflecting telescope, perhaps with a mirror as great as 600 inches (15 m) into space. Such a telescope would be free of Earth's distorting atmosphere and also its gravity, which deforms telescope mirrors and limits their size. The many uses Spitzer saw for a space telescope

---

SOCIAL IMPACT: FUSION POWER

Some scientists believe that the research of Lyman Spitzer and others on plasmas and controlled atomic fusion will someday lead to an abundant, nonpolluting source of energy. Unlike today's nuclear power plants, which gain their energy from atomic fission, fusion plants would produce no radioactive waste. Engineers theorize that the plants could be built in such a way that the laws of physics would shut them down in case of a failure, so the plants would be completely safe. Fusion plants would not release carbon dioxide or other greenhouse gases, so fusion power would not contribute to global warming. Hydrogen, the fuel that such plants would use, exists in essentially infinite supply.

Unfortunately, the goal of producing useful energy from atomic fusion seems almost as far off today as it did when Spitzer pursued it in the 1950s. Achieving the extremely high temperature and density of protons needed for a fusion reaction and containing the plasma in which the reaction would take place have proved almost impossible.

So far, a magnetic field seems the best "bottle" for the plasma. The most common type of experimental fusion reactor that uses magnetic fields is the tokamak, first developed in Russia in 1969. Even the best tokamaks have not quite achieved the break-even point, where they produce more energy than is required to start them up. They are even further from the ignition stage, in which the reaction produces enough energy to sustain itself in spite of the losses that unavoidably occur, including the removal of energy for human use.

Researchers also continue to explore plasma container designs other than tokamaks, including descendants of Spitzer's Stellarator. Spitzer wrote in 1997 that he thought a Stellarator might be less expensive than a tokamak. In late 2004, the Princeton Plasma Physics Laboratory, with the support of the U.S. Department of Energy, was working on a project called the National Compact Stellarator Experiment.

included finding out the structure of star clusters and galaxies, the nature of other planets, and the size of the universe. But, he wrote, "the chief contribution of such a radically new and . . . powerful instrument . . . would be . . . to uncover new phenomena not yet imagined, and perhaps modify profoundly our basic concepts of space and time."

RAND did nothing about Spitzer's suggestions, but the idea of a telescope in space took a strong hold on Spitzer himself. "Working for such a project became for me a major long-term objective," he wrote in *Dreams, Stars, and Electrons*. He would continue to pursue that objective for more than 40 years and would live to see many of the activities he had proposed in his report carried out by the *Hubble Space Telescope*. "I regard as my major contribution to HST [the *Hubble Space Telescope*] that decade after decade, before the official start, I continued actively to push this long-range program," Spitzer concluded.

Progress in Space

Events during the next two decades began bringing Spitzer's vision closer to reality. The Soviet Union sent the first space satellite, *Sputnik I,* into Earth's orbit on October 4, 1957. A year later, the United States established the National Aeronautics and Space Administration (NASA) to handle its own satellite launching and space exploration program.

Study committees from the National Academy of Sciences, all of which included Spitzer, recommended to NASA in 1962, 1965, and 1968 that the space agency sponsor creation of a large space telescope. At first the committees saw such a telescope only as a long-range goal. When the government approved development of the space shuttle in 1972, however, a space telescope began to look more practical. Able to make repeated round trips into space, shuttles not only could bring the telescope into Earth orbit but also could allow astronauts on later trips to repair and upgrade the device, thus greatly prolonging its useful life.

During this same period, Spitzer was working on space research of his own. Beginning in 1962, Spitzer, along with others at Princeton, helped to develop one of four Orbiting Astronomical Observatories sponsored by NASA. This satellite, eventually named *Copernicus,* contained a 32-inch (81-cm) telescope attached to a spectroscope that recorded ultraviolet radiation. Launched in 1972, *Copernicus* remained in operation until 1981. Spitzer used its data to discover that interstellar gas was not spread out evenly between the stars, as astronomers had thought. Rather, the gas was clumped into dense clouds alternating with jets of hotter, thinner material thrown out by supernovas.

Struggles for Support

Lyman Spitzer found that persuading fellow astronomers and NASA officials to share his enthusiasm for a space telescope was an uphill battle. Many of his colleagues feared that a space telescope project would take money from the building of larger Earth-based telescopes, which they preferred. Some doubted whether a telescope in space could be kept steady enough to make useful observations. Slowly, however, Spitzer made headway. By 1974, he could write (in a paper reprinted in *Dreams, Stars, and Electrons*) that "the LST [Large Space Telescope] seems to be an idea whose time has come."

Spitzer's next task, talking Congress into funding the project, was no less difficult. Between 1975 and 1977, he urged astronomers who had come to share his dream to write letters to their senators and representatives. In addition, he and fellow telescope supporter John Bahcall, an astrophysicist at Princeton's Institute for Advanced Study, buttonholed members of Congress wherever they could catch them. Through several anxious years, funding was canceled, restored, and canceled again as the economy and congressional opinions swung back and forth. Finally, however, largely because of Spitzer's and Bahcall's efforts, Congress approved money for the program in 1977.

The space telescope was built during the late 1970s and early 1980s. Perkin-Elmer Corporation, an instrument-making company in Danbury, Connecticut, completed the telescope's 94-inch (2.4-m) primary mirror in 1981, and the cameras, spectroscopes, and other instruments that would accompany the telescope were finished in

1983. The space telescope, by then named after astronomy pioneer Edwin Hubble, was fully assembled, at a cost of $2.1 billion, in 1985. The telescope was scheduled to be launched in 1986, but the explosion of the space shuttle *Challenger* early that year grounded all shuttle flights for four years.

A Disastrous Mistake

The *Hubble Space Telescope* finally was carried into orbit aboard the space shuttle *Discovery* on April 24, 1990—54 years after Lyman Spitzer had first proposed building a telescope in space. Spitzer and his family watched the launch and found it "tremendously exciting," he wrote in *Dreams, Stars, and Electrons*.

The Hubble Space Telescope, *launched in 1990, has allowed astronomers to obtain views of the universe that would never have been possible on Earth. (NASA/Space Telescope Science Institute)*

Within a few months, however, the scientists studying the telescope's first images noticed a huge problem. Perkin-Elmer apparently had made a mistake in casting *Hubble's* main mirror, creating an optical defect called spherical aberration. The mirror was too flat near the edge by a mere 0.05 inch (1.3 mm), about 1/50th the width of a human hair, but this seemingly tiny error made most of the telescope's images hopelessly blurry. Spitzer learned about this disaster on his 76th birthday—"an unexpected and certainly a most unwelcome present," he recalled.

The difficulty looked incurable at first, and the much-praised telescope seemed doomed to be almost useless. After a year or so, however, Spitzer and other scientists designed lenses to correct the problem. Astronauts installed the lenses, along with other equipment replacements and upgrades, on December 2, 1993. After that, the telescope performed almost perfectly for more than 10 years. "We went from

---

SOLVING PROBLEMS: CONTACT LENSES FOR A TELESCOPE

At first, the scientists trying to correct the flaw in the *Hubble Space Telescope's* mirror could not agree on how to go about it. Making and installing a new primary mirror was out of the question. Some members of the group thought that corrective lenses should be placed on the main telescope. Lyman Spitzer, however, recommended creating a corrective lens—in essence, prescription glasses or contact lenses—for each of the telescope's instruments.

In the end, the telescope group developed two devices to solve their problem. One was a new version of one of the telescope's original instruments, the wide-field/planetary camera. The revised camera sent light from Hubble's large mirror to relay mirrors shaped to compensate for the error in the main mirror. The relay mirrors made up the second device, the Corrective Optics Space Telescope Axial Replacement (COSTAR). These mirrors transmitted the light, now properly focused, to the individual Hubble instruments.

Over time, astronauts replaced all of the telescope's original instruments. The new instruments had corrective optics built in, so COSTAR was no longer needed.

being called a national disgrace . . . to being an icon of American know-how and technology," Ed Weiler, the Hubble project's chief scientist, told Eric Levin in 2003. "It [was] quite a roller-coaster ride."

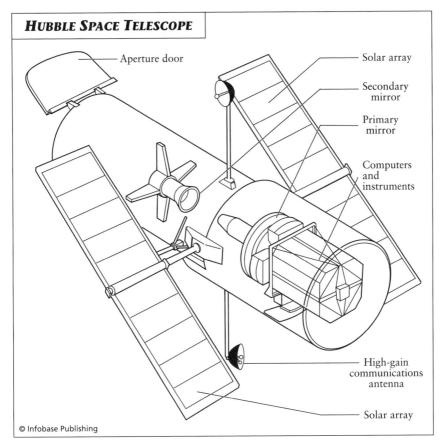

HUBBLE SPACE TELESCOPE

Aperture door

Solar array

Secondary mirror

Primary mirror

Computers and instruments

High-gain communications antenna

Solar array

© Infobase Publishing

The Hubble Space Telescope, *powered by winglike solar panels and steered by onboard computers, contains a 94-inch (2.4-m) primary mirror, a secondary mirror, and five instruments: the Advanced Camera for Surveys (ACS), the Wide Field and Planetary Camera 2 (WFPC2), the Near Infrared Camera and Multi-Object Spectrometer (NICMOS), the Space Telescope Imaging Spectrograph (STIS), and the Fine Guidance Sensors (FGS). The Wide Field and Planetary Camera is the most important of these. The Fine Guidance Sensors help to keep the telescope pointed at particular stars or other objects.*

Amazing *Hubble*

When waves of light or other radiation enter the *Hubble Space Telescope,* they first strike its large primary mirror. That mirror reflects the radiation onto a smaller secondary mirror, which focuses it and bounces it back toward the primary one. The waves of radiation pass through a hole in the primary mirror and are focused again on a spot behind the mirror. There, smaller mirrors that are half reflective and half transparent send the radiation to the fine guidance sensors that keep the telescope aligned with targets chosen from Earth and to the four scientific instruments located behind the mirror.

The most important of the telescope's instruments, the wide-field/ planetary camera, can examine large areas of space at low resolution or, alternatively, make high-resolution images of planets in the solar system. Instead of photographic film, it uses charge-coupled devices (CCDs), solid-state detectors that produce a small electric charge when struck by light or ultraviolet rays. Film picks up only about 1 percent of the light that falls on it, whereas CCDs register almost all the light. The detectors' electrical signals are stored in an onboard computer and then relayed to Earth, where they can be analyzed and transformed into visual images. *Hubble*'s other instruments are the near-infrared camera and multi-object spectrometer, the space telescope imaging spectrograph, and the advanced camera for surveys.

The *Hubble Space Telescope*'s many achievements include new discoveries about the size and age of the universe, the evolution of stars and galaxies, the birth and death of stars, the formation and existence of planets orbiting other stars, and black holes. In 1994, for example, the telescope helped astronomers prove the existence of supermassive black holes, and a survey of 27 nearby galaxies made by *Hubble* in 1997 showed that such black holes probably exist in the centers of most large galaxies. Measurements released in 1999, based on data from *Hubble,* indicated that the universe is between 12 and 14 billion years old. *Hubble* photos have also shown that pancake-shaped disks of dust around young stars are common and have revealed that planets are forming in some of these disks.

Few astronomers would question that the *Hubble Space Telescope* has revolutionized their science. "Before the telescope there were optical astronomers, radio astronomers, X-ray astronomers, UV [ultraviolet light] astronomers, theoretical astronomers, infrared astronomers," John Bahcall said to Christopher Tyner of *Investor's Business Daily.* "Now there are just astronomers . . . [because] every-

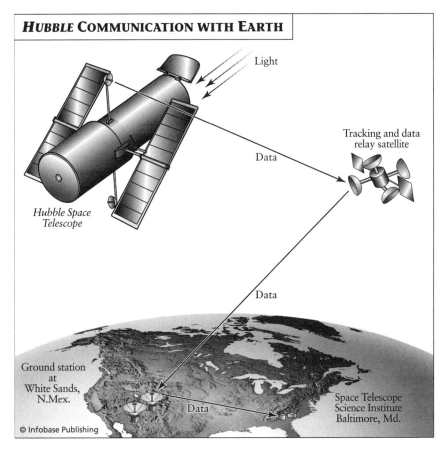

HUBBLE COMMUNICATION WITH EARTH

Light

Tracking and data relay satellite

Data

Hubble Space Telescope

Data

Ground station at White Sands, N.Mex.

Data

Space Telescope Science Institute Baltimore, Md.

© Infobase Publishing

The Hubble Space Telescope *communicates with Earth by a somewhat indirect path. Digital data gathered by the telescope and its instruments are sent from the spacecraft's two communication antennas to a tracking and data relay satellite. The satellite, in turn, broadcasts to a ground station at White Sands, New Mexico. The ground station transmits its information to the Goddard Space Flight Center in Greenbelt, Maryland. Finally, Goddard passes the data to the Space Telescope Science Institute in Baltimore, where computers and scientists analyze it.*

body has understood that they need the *Hubble Space Telescope* to study their kind of object."

A Distinguished Career

While the *Hubble Space Telescope* was being built and, later, was providing a wealth of new information to astronomers including himself, Lyman Spitzer was continuing his scientific career. During the 1970s and 1980s, he won numerous awards from both inside and outside the United States. His U.S. awards included the Catherine Wolfe Bruce Medal from the Astronomical Society of the Pacific (1973), the Henry Draper Medal from the National Academy of Sciences (1974), and the American Physical Society's first James Clerk Maxwell Prize for plasma physics (1975). NASA gave him a Distinguished Public Service Medal in 1976, and President Jimmy Carter awarded him the National Medal of Science in 1979. Spitzer also won Germany's Karl Schwartzschild Medal in 1975, the Gold Medal of Britain's Royal Astronomical Society in 1978, and the Jules Janssen Medal of the Société Astronomique de France in 1978. Spitzer's most prestigious award was the Royal Swedish Academy's Crafoord Prize, which he won in 1985. This prize is considered the equivalent of the Nobel Prize in fields not eligible for the Nobel.

Lyman Spitzer was highly regarded as a teacher, an author, and a person. A 2003 NASA article about Spitzer said that his colleagues described him as a man of "incredible discipline, diligence, and politeness." In an obituary article published in *Physics Today,* John Bahcall and Jeremiah P. Ostriker, Spitzer's successor as head of the Princeton astrophysics department and observatory, wrote, "Lyman Spitzer lived a graceful life, exuding dignity and fairness. He was admired and loved by all who knew him."

Space Telescope Legacy

In 2004, Congress decided that the *Hubble Space Telescope* had fulfilled its useful life, which had been predicted to be 10 to 20 years, and refused to allocate funds for a space shuttle mission to repair it. This decision no doubt would have greatly disappointed Lyman Spitzer, but Spitzer did not live to see it. After a day spent partly in analyzing *Hubble Space Telescope* data, he died suddenly at his home on March 31, 1997, at the age of 82.

In addition to the awards Spitzer received during his lifetime, NASA honored Spitzer after his death by naming a new astronomical satellite after him. The *Spitzer Space Telescope,* launched on August 25, 2003, contains instruments that collect infrared and near-infrared radiation. This telescope is especially well suited to see through the dust around stars and galaxies, a subject that always interested Spitzer. It has revealed much about the way stars and planets form.

Spitzer also would be pleased to know that, although his beloved telescope will soon go out of operation, other space telescopes will replace it. The largest one planned is the *James Webb Space Telescope,* which will have a mirror 20 feet (6.5 m) in diameter. Like the smaller *Spitzer Space Telescope,* it will detect radiation in the infrared and near-infrared range. This telescope, scheduled for launch in 2011, will study the earliest stars and galaxies formed after the big bang. These objects' high redshift moves most of their radiation into the infrared by the time it reaches Earth.

Lyman Spitzer himself is sure to be remembered. Christopher Tyner quoted Spitzer as saying that he had a "fascination with the spectacular," and Spitzer's own achievements, like those of the telescope he helped to establish, were spectacular indeed.

Chronology

1914	Lyman Spitzer, Jr., born in Toledo, Ohio, on June 26
1935	Spitzer earns B.S. in physics from Yale University
1938	Spitzer earns Princeton University's first Ph.D. degree in theoretical astrophysics
1939	Spitzer joins faculty of Yale
1942–46	Spitzer helps to develop sonar during World War II

1946	Spitzer proposes development of a large space telescope and lists its scientific uses
1947	Spitzer becomes head of the Princeton astrophysics department and director of the university's astronomical observatory
1951	Spitzer designs the Stellarator, a possible device for containing a controlled atomic fusion reaction; he persuades the Atomic Energy Commission to fund a project on controlled thermonuclear fusion at Princeton
1952	Spitzer becomes Charles A. Young Professor of Astronomy at Princeton
1957	Russia launches first artificial satellite, *Sputnik 1,* on October 4
1958	Princeton's fusion energy project becomes the Princeton Plasma Physics Laboratory, with Spitzer as its director; U.S. government establishes National Aeronautics and Space Administration (NASA)
1960s	Three committees from the National Academy of Sciences recommend that NASA sponsor development of a space telescope; Spitzer tries to convince fellow astronomers that a space telescope could be valuable
1962	Spitzer begins helping to develop *Copernicus,* an Orbiting Astronomical Observatory that records ultraviolet radiation
1967	Spitzer resigns as head of plasma physics laboratory
1972	Government approves development of space shuttle; *Copernicus* satellite launched
1975–77	Spitzer and John Bahcall attempt to persuade Congress to fund the NASA space telescope project
1977	Congress approves funding for the Large Space Telescope
1979	Spitzer wins National Medal of Science; he steps down as head of Princeton's astrophysics department and director of the astronomical observatory
1981	Perkin-Elmer Corporation completes space telescope's primary mirror

1982	Spitzer retires from Princeton faculty at age 68
1983	Scientific instruments for space telescope completed
1985	Space telescope assembled; Spitzer wins Crafoord Prize
1986	Explosion of space shuttle *Challenger* grounds all shuttle flights for four years, delaying launch of the space telescope
1990	The space shuttle *Discovery* carries the *Hubble Space Telescope* into orbit on April 24; scientists discover that a mistake in shaping the telescope's primary mirror is making most of its images blurry
1990–93	Corrective lenses for the telescope are designed
1993	Astronauts place corrective lenses in the telescope on December 2
1997	Spitzer dies on March 31
1999	Measurements from the *Hubble Space Telescope* allow astronomers to determine the age of the universe
2003	*Spitzer Space Telescope* launched on August 25
2004	Congress refuses to grant funding for repairs for *Hubble Space Telescope*

Further Reading

Books

Spitzer, Lyman, Jr., and Jeremiah P. Ostriker, eds. *Dreams, Stars, and Electrons: Selected Writings of Lyman Spitzer, Jr.* Princeton, N.J.: Princeton University Press, 1997.
> Reprints of Spitzer's most important scientific papers, accompanied by Spitzer's comments, some of which are autobiographical.

Tucker, Wallace, and Karen Tucker. *Modern Telescopes and Their Makers.* Cambridge, Mass.: Harvard University Press, 1986.
> Includes a chapter on the early development of the space telescope.

Articles

Bahcall, John N., and Jeremiah P. Ostriker. "Lyman Spitzer, Jr." *Physics Today* 50 (October 1997): 123–124.
Obituary by two men who knew Spitzer well.
Freudenrich, Craig. "How Hubble Space Telescope Works." Howstuffworks Web site. Available online. URL: http://science. howstuffworks.com/hubble1.htm. Accessed on February 5, 2005.
This well-illustrated article explains the telescope's history, its optics and scientific instruments, and its spacecraft systems.
HubbleSite.org. "About Hubble." Hubble Space Telescope Web site. Available online. URL: http://hubblesite.org/newscenter/ news_media_resources/reference_center/about_hubble. Accessed on February 4, 2005.
Includes facts about the space telescope, its impact on astronomy, and its greatest discoveries.
Kincade, Kathy. "Space-based Telescopes Take Astronomers Places They Have Never Gone Before." *Laser Focus World* 40 (September 2004): 83–86.
Discusses the advantages of space-based over Earth-based telescopes and describes the *Hubble Space Telescope* and its descendants, including the *Spitzer Space Telescope* and the *James Webb Space Telescope*.
Levin, Eric. "Ed Weiler." *Discover* 24 (November 2003): 44–48.
Introduces Ed Weiler, NASA's chief of space science and chief scientist on the Hubble project from 1979 to 1998. Explains Weiler's role in the telescope's launch and development, including repair of a flaw in its primary mirror.
Kennedy Space Center. "NASA Space Shuttle Mission STS-31 Press Kit." Available online. URL: http://science.ksc.nasa.gov/ shuttle/missions/sts-31/sts-31-press-kit.txt. Accessed on February 4, 2005.
Press kit for the mission that launched the *Hubble Space Telescope* in April 1990; includes information about the telescope's history, a detailed description of the telescope and its instruments, astronomical questions the telescope was designed to answer, a chronology of the expected mission, and a list of groups involved with the telescope's development and use.

Spitzer Space Telescope Web site. "Lyman Spitzer, Jr." Available online. URL: http://www.spitzer.caltech.edu/about/spitzer.shtml. Accessed on January 30, 2005.

Concise biography of Spitzer, posted by NASA and the California Institute of Technology when the *Spitzer Space Telescope* was launched in 2003.

Tyner, Christopher L. "Astronomer Lyman Spitzer—His Drive Helped Put the Universe in Focus." *Investor's Business Daily,* July 7, 2000: A03.

This short biographical piece about Spitzer includes many quotes and anecdotes.

Web Sites

Amazing Space. URL: http://amazing-space.stsci.edu. Accessed on February 4, 2005.

Educational site sponsored by the Space Telescope Science Institute's Office of Public Outreach. It includes online explorations, news, links, and homework help related to the *Hubble Space Telescope.*

HubbleSite. URL: http://hubblesite.org. Accessed on February 4, 2005.

The official Web site of the *Hubble Space Telescope.* It includes a news center, a gallery, information about *Hubble's* discoveries, illustrated descriptions of how the telescope and its instruments work, interactive games and activities for students, and reference information about the telescope.

8

THE INVISIBLE UNIVERSE

VERA RUBIN AND DARK MATTER

"The world is not only stranger than we suppose, but stranger than we can suppose," British evolutionary biologist J. B. S. Haldane once said. Astronomers, like researchers in other branches of science, have learned Haldane's lesson over and over as they discovered aspects of the universe that earlier scientists never imagined.

In the 1970s and early 1980s, astronomers discovered once again how little they really knew about the cosmos. Compelling evidence showed that all their telescopes put together could observe only 5 to 10 percent of the matter in the universe; all the rest is "dark," seemingly giving off no radiation at all. This shocking finding came from an unlikely source: an astronomer not trained in any of the usual colleges, not working on any of the science's popular topics, and—most unusual of all—not a man. The scientist who first proved the existence of what has come to be called dark matter was one of the era's few women astronomers, Vera (Cooper) Rubin.

Window on the Stars

The view from Vera Cooper's bedroom window first drew her to the stars. She was born in Philadelphia on July 23, 1928, and spent her early years in Mount Airy, Pennsylvania. When Vera was 10 years old, however, her parents, Philip and Rose Cooper, moved with her

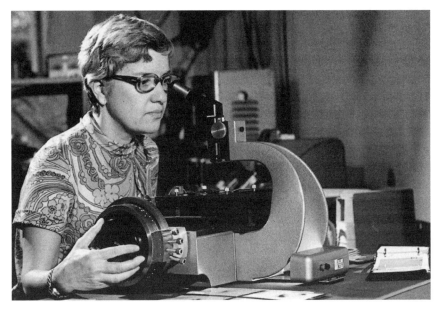

By measuring how fast stars in different parts of galaxies were rotating around the galaxies' centers, Vera Rubin discovered that most of the matter in the universe cannot be seen. (Carnegie Institution of Washington)

and her older sister, Ruth, to Washington, D.C. Vera's bed was under a north-facing window in her new home, and she often lay awake at night, watching the stars slowly wheel across the dark sky as the Earth turned. From that time on, she wanted to be an astronomer.

Vera Cooper wanted to attend Vassar College, a small, all-female school in Poughkeepsie, New York, because Maria Mitchell, the first prominent woman astronomer in the United States, had taught there in the mid-19th century. A second reason for going to Vassar was that "I needed a scholarship, and they gave me one," as she told *Mercury* assistant editor Sally Stephens in a 1991 interview (reprinted in Vera Rubin's collection of papers, *Bright Galaxies, Dark Matters*). Vassar hardly specialized in astronomy during Cooper's time; however, she was the only astronomy major in her class.

The summer before Cooper graduated from Vassar, a new interest entered her life. Her parents introduced her to Robert (Bob) Rubin, a student in physical chemistry at Cornell University in Ithaca, New York. Vera Cooper and Bob Rubin married in 1948, right after Cooper graduated from Vassar.

Circling Galaxies

At the time, Bob Rubin was still working on his Ph.D. at Cornell. Most married scientists in those days automatically saw the man's career as more important than the woman's, so Vera Rubin concluded that she, too, should take her advanced training at Cornell, even though the university's astronomy department consisted of only two people. In fact, she did not have many other choices. The dean of Princeton's graduate school, for instance, refused to mail her a catalog of the school's programs because, he informed her, Princeton's graduate astronomy program did not accept women.

Because Bob Rubin's Ph.D. research was already partly completed and the couple would probably move when it was finished, Vera Rubin knew she would not be at Cornell long enough to obtain her own doctoral degree. She therefore signed up for a master's degree program instead. For her master's thesis, Rubin decided, after discussions with her husband, to examine the motions of all galaxies with known velocities to see if they had a systematic pattern of motion besides that due to the expansion of the universe.

Most master's thesis projects make no great scientific waves, but Rubin's reached a startling conclusion: Galaxies at about the same distance from the Milky Way were moving faster in some parts of the sky than others. This fact suggested that the galaxies were rotating around an unknown center, just as the planets in the solar system rotate around the Sun.

Rubin presented her work in a 10-minute talk at a meeting of the American Astronomical Society in Philadelphia in December 1950, only a few weeks after she earned her master's degree and gave birth to her first child, David. Few astronomers accepted her conclusions at the time, but later research showed that she was right. Indeed, her study helped another astronomer, Gerard de Vaucouleurs, develop the idea of galaxy superclusters—large collections of smaller galaxy groups and clusters—which are among the largest structures in the universe.

A Lumpy Cosmos

Their studies at Cornell completed, Vera and Bob Rubin moved to Washington, D.C., in 1951. Bob began working at the Applied Physics Laboratory of Johns Hopkins University, but Vera stayed at home with David. Her chance of having a career in astronomy seemed to be fading away. Every time she read a new issue of the *Astrophysical Journal,* she said later, she burst into tears.

Bob Rubin could not stand to see his wife so unhappy. In 1952, he encouraged Vera to begin studying for her doctorate at Georgetown University, the only college in the area with a Ph.D. program in astronomy. Vera did not drive, so Bob drove her to evening classes and waited in the car to take her home. Vera's parents, who still lived in Washington, stayed with her children. (By then the Rubins also had a daughter, Judith.) "We did that two nights a week for about a year," Rubin recalled to Lisa Yount in 1994. "It was a . . . three-ring circus."

Around this time, Bob introduced Vera to astrophysicist Ralph Asher Alpher, with whom he shared an office at the Applied Physics Laboratory. Alpher was just becoming famous for his work with Russian-born cosmologist George Gamow on the theory that the universe began with a gigantic explosion, later termed the *big bang.* Alpher, in turn, introduced the Rubins to Gamow.

Gamow was very interested in the research Vera Rubin had done for her master's thesis, and he sometimes called her to discuss astronomical topics. During one call, Gamow asked whether there might be a pattern in the distribution of galaxies in space. Rubin decided that this would make a fine topic for her Ph.D. thesis. Gamow agreed, and he became her thesis adviser, even though he taught at George Washington University rather than Georgetown. "My entire . . . thesis consisted of essentially one very long [mathematical] calculation," Rubin told Lisa Yount. Rubin said that a computer could do the same calculation today in only a few hours, but at the time, using a desktop calculator, she spent more than a year performing it.

Once again, Rubin's results surprised everyone. Most astronomers had assumed that galaxies would be distributed evenly or randomly, but Rubin found a pattern in their distribution: Galaxies tended to occur in clusters, which in turn made up still larger clusters. As with her earlier work on galaxy motion, her conclusions attracted little attention at the time, but about 15 years later, other researchers confirmed her discovery. Rubin earned her Ph.D. from Georgetown in 1954.

After a year of teaching physics and mathematics at Montgomery County Community College, Rubin began researching and, eventually, teaching at Georgetown. She also continued raising her family, which came to include four children. All four grew up to obtain Ph.D.s in science—two in geology, one in mathematics, and one in astronomy. "We lived in a household where being a scientist looked like so much fun," Judith Rubin Young told *Science* reporter Robert Irion in 2002. "How could we possibly want to do anything else?" Vera Rubin has said she is as proud of her children and of her ability to combine a career with raising a family as she is of her scientific achievements.

Exploring the Outer Stars

A project that Rubin assigned to one of her classes at Georgetown was the first step on the path that led her to her greatest discovery. With her students as collaborators, she attempted to find out how fast stars in the outer parts of the Milky Way were rotating around the galaxy's center. Although speeds of rotation had been determined for stars near the center, she found that very little information existed about the behavior of stars near the galaxy's wispy edges. Around 1963, Rubin decided to fill in this gap in astronomers' knowledge by making her own observations of the outer stars.

Rubin made her first observations at Kitt Peak National Observatory in Arizona. A well-known husband-and-wife team of astronomers, Geoffrey and Margaret Burbidge, then invited her to join them in observing at the McDonald Observatory in Texas.

Finally, in 1965, Rubin took her research to George Ellery Hale's famous observatory at Mount Palomar, California, where she became the first woman legally permitted to use the 200-inch (5-m) Hale Telescope.

The Burbidges' encouragement made Rubin bold enough to take a step she had been thinking about for many years. When she was working on her Ph.D. thesis, she and George Gamow had sometimes met in the wood-paneled library of the Department of Terrestrial Magnetism (DTM) of the Carnegie Institution of Washington, one of five institutions that Andrew Carnegie, the steel magnate, had established during the early years of the 20th century. (George Ellery Hale's Mount Wilson Observatory was another.) Rubin liked the supportive atmosphere at the DTM and hoped that she would someday work there. By 1965, she felt that she had enough experience to persuade the DTM to hire her, so she asked the institution for a job. The DTM was primarily a geophysics laboratory at the time, but its administrators nonetheless granted Rubin's request. She has remained at the DTM ever since, and several other astronomers have joined her there.

A Surprise in Andromeda

After Rubin joined the DTM, she learned that one of the institution's staff scientists, Kent Ford, had recently built a spectrograph connected to an image tube. This new invention enhanced images of spectra electronically, allowing observations to be made of much fainter and more distant objects than had been possible before. Rubin began working with Ford soon after she joined the DTM.

At first, Rubin and Ford used the image tube spectrograph to study quasars. Rubin soon gave up this project, however, because so many other astronomers were researching quasars. "I didn't like working on problems that many other people were working on and where I was constantly being beseiged with questions about the work," she told Sally Stephens in 1991. "So I decided to pick a program that no one would care about while I was doing it. But, at the same time, one that the astronomical community would be very happy with when I was done."

Eleanor Margaret Peachey Burbidge has won fame both in her native England and in the United States. She was born in Davenport, England, on August 12, 1919. Like Vera Rubin, Margaret Peachey, as she was then known, became interested in astronomy by watching the stars as a child. She first remembers being fascinated by them when she saw them through the porthole of a ship crossing the English Channel when she was four years old.

Peachey earned a bachelor's degree in astronomy from University College, part of the University of London, in 1939 and a Ph.D. from the University of London Observatory in 1943. While taking further classes at University College in the late 1940s, she met Geoffrey Burbidge, who was then studying physics. They married in 1948. Geoffrey Burbidge soon also became an astronomer.

The Burbidges first became famous in the early 1950s, when they worked with British astronomer Fred Hoyle and nuclear physicist William Fowler to develop a theory explaining how all the chemical elements could be made in stars and broadcast into space by supernova explosions. The four scientists' proposal, published in 1953 under the

---

Rubin decided to extend her earlier Milky Way research to stars in other galaxies. She hoped that learning how fast stars in different parts of galaxies are rotating might help her understand why galaxies have different shapes and how these giant clusters of stars formed and evolved. In 1970, she and Ford began making spectra of stars and gas clouds in different parts of the Andromeda galaxy, or M31, the first "nebula" that Edwin Hubble had shown to lie outside the Milky Way.

Like so much of Vera Rubin's research, this project produced an unexpected result. The laws of gravity state that when a small mass orbits or rotates around a larger mass, the small mass will rotate faster if it is close to the large mass than it will if it is far away. That fact explains why the planets in the solar system nearest the Sun, such as Mercury, move faster in their orbits than more distant planets, such as Saturn or Pluto. Most of the light

title "Synthesis of the Elements in Stars," became known as the B^{2}FH theory, for the first letters of the scientists' last names (fellow researchers had nicknamed the Burbidges, who often worked together, "B squared").

In the early 1960s, Margaret Burbidge, then teaching with her husband at the University of California, San Diego, became interested in the motions of stars and gas clouds within galaxies. When she found that she shared this interest with Vera Rubin, she encouraged the younger woman's research. Both Burbidge and Rubin measured velocities of gas clouds and other material in different parts of galaxies from spectra taken at the McDonald Observatory in Texas during the early and mid-1960s. Much of Burbidge's later research focused on quasars.

Margaret Burbidge has received numerous honors, including the Warner Prize in Astronomy (1959) and the Gold Medal of the Royal Astronomical Society of London (2005), both shared with her husband. She has also held many prestigious positions, including the directorship of Britain's Royal Greenwich Observatory (1972–73) and the presidency of the American Astronomical Society (1976–78). She was the first woman to hold either of these posts. Like Vera Rubin, Burbidge has made a point of encouraging other women to enter astronomy.

in Andromeda is in its central bulge, so everyone assumed that most of the galaxy's mass was in its center as well. If that was true, stars and gas in Andromeda's outer fringes should rotate more slowly than those near its center. To their amazement, however, Rubin and Ford found that material in the outer parts of Andromeda was rotating about as fast as that in the inner parts—and sometimes faster.

The Rubin-Ford Effect

Rubin and Ford could think of no explanation for their astounding finding, and neither could other astronomers. Once again, many of Vera Rubin's peers disbelieved her work, and once again, because she did not like controversy, Rubin decided to study something

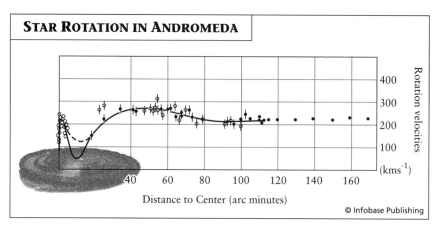

STAR ROTATION IN ANDROMEDA

400
300
200
100
(kms⁻¹)

Rotation velocities

40   60   80   100   120   140   160

Distance to Center (arc minutes)

© Infobase Publishing

Vera Rubin found that stars and gas in the outer part of the Andromeda galaxy (M31) were rotating around the galaxy's center much faster than expected. This result indicated that the galaxy had to be surrounded by a halo of "dark" (invisible) matter whose gravity was affecting the stars' motion. The stars' speed, shown along the right side of the diagram, is measured in kilometers per second. The solid and dashed lines are based on optical observations by Rubin and Kent Ford. The triangular points in the far right side of the diagram come from radio observations made in 1975 by two other scientists, Roberts and Whitehurst.

different for the time being. She and Ford therefore returned to the puzzling discovery she had made at Cornell, the fact that large groups of galaxies seemed to have motions besides those predicted by the theory of the expanding universe.

Rubin and Ford found large-scale motions among groups of galaxies, using more galaxies and more exact measurements than had been possible before. They also found that the "local group" of galaxies, which includes the Milky Way and Andromeda, is being pulled across the universe as a unit. This additional motion became known as the Rubin-Ford effect.

Later studies have confirmed that in many parts of space, groups of galaxies move together toward regions where galaxies are packed more tightly, drawn by the gravity of these denser regions. This phenomenon, called large-scale streaming, contributes to the "lumpiness" in distribution of matter that Rubin and others have observed.

Invisible Halos

Rubin and Ford returned to their work on rotational velocities in the mid-1970s, this time studying galaxies more distant than M31. Because these galaxies appeared smaller than Andromeda, the scientists could observe a "slice" going clear across one of the galaxies in just a few hours. These galaxies showed the same results that Rubin and Ford had seen earlier in the Andromeda galaxy. In fact, the pair found that stars in the outer parts of the galaxies were moving so fast that they would escape the galaxies' gravity and fly off into space—unless a great deal of invisible matter was providing still more gravity to hold them in place. In time, Rubin, Ford, and other DTM astronomers confirmed these findings in a wide variety of galaxies.

By the early 1980s, astronomers had to admit that Rubin's discovery was real and face its astonishing implication: Either the laws of gravity worked differently on this cosmic scale than at more ordinary distances (which seemed highly unlikely), or galaxies' mass was not distributed in the same way as their light. Only a very large mass of invisible material, forming a more or less spherical halo around a galaxy, could provide the gravity needed to maintain the rotation of the galaxy's outer stars at the speeds Ford and Rubin observed. This dark matter, as it came to be called, had to have a mass 10 times as great as that of the visible galaxy.

Cosmologist Fritz Zwicky and astronomer Sinclair Smith had predicted the existence of dark matter in the 1930s after noting that galaxies in certain clusters were moving relative to each other so fast that the clusters should have broken up, yet the groups remained intact. Other explanations for this observation were possible, so most astronomers had not found Zwicky and Smith's proposal convincing. Only Rubin's work, because it covered so many galaxies and was done so carefully, persuaded them that the earlier theory had been correct. Data from radio telescopes and Riccardo Giacconi's *Einstein* X-ray satellite provided further confirmation of dark matter's existence around 1980.

Most astronomers now believe that 90 to 95 percent of the universe's mass is undetectable except through its gravitational effects. Only a small fraction of this material can be "conventional" matter such as black holes, large planets, or dim stars called white dwarfs. Most of it must consist of unknown types of subatomic particles or other unconventional matter.

Enormous Fun

While others speculate about dark matter, Vera Rubin goes on watching the stars—and making new discoveries. In the early 1990s, for instance, she found a strange galaxy in which half the stars are rotating clockwise and the other half counterclockwise. She thinks this galaxy obtained some of its stars when it merged with a cloud of gas. Her discovery provides evidence for the idea, proposed by others, that large galaxies form from combinations of smaller galaxies and gas clouds. Rubin has done other research on the evolution of galaxies with her daughter, Judith Young, a professor of astronomy at the University of Massachusetts, Amherst.

Remembering her own struggles for acceptance, Vera Rubin has worked hard to improve women's access to careers in astronomy. "I'm satisfied that [the chance for women to have a successful career in astronomy is] improving," she told Sally Stephens in 1991, although she admitted that "it really is improving very, very slowly." Rubin encourages young women interested in astronomy or any other science to "absolutely not give up." She reminds them that, with luck and support, they can have both a family and a career, as she herself has done so successfully.

Rubin has won many honors for her work, including election to the National Academy of Sciences (1981), the National Medal of Science (1993), the Gold Medal of the Royal Astronomical Society (1996), the Cosmology Prize of the Peter Gruber Foundation (2002), and the Astronomical Society of the Pacific's Bruce Medal (2003). She was the first woman to be awarded the Royal Astronomical Society's Gold Medal since famed 19th-century astronomer Caroline Herschel received it in 1828.

Far more than awards, however, Rubin treasures the process of doing research. "It's enormous fun," she said in the interview with Stephens. "Observing is spectacularly lovely. . . . And I enjoy analyzing the observations, trying to see what you have, trying to understand what you're learning. . . . What keeps me going is . . . hope and curiosity, this basic curiosity about how the universe works."

Chronology

1928	Vera Cooper born in Philadelphia on July 23
1930s	Fritz Zwicky and Sinclair Smith predict existence of dark matter
1938	Cooper family moves to Washington, D.C., and Vera Cooper begins watching the stars through her bedroom window
1948	Cooper graduates from Vassar with bachelor's degree in astronomy and marries Robert (Bob) Rubin
1950	Vera Rubin obtains master's degree from Cornell University in November; she gives talk to American Astronomical Society meeting in December, reporting that galaxies appear to be rotating around a common center
1951	The Rubins move to Washington, D.C.
1952	Vera Rubin begins studying for Ph.D. at Georgetown University
1954	Rubin concludes that galaxies are distributed unevenly in the universe; she earns a Ph.D. from Georgetown
1955–64	Rubin researches and teaches at Georgetown; with her husband, she raises four children
1963	Rubin begins observing to determine rotation speeds of stars in the outer parts of the Milky Way
1965	Rubin becomes first woman legally allowed to use telescope at Mount Palomar; she joins Department of Terrestrial Magnetism, a research laboratory of the Carnegie Institution of Washington
1970	Rubin and Kent Ford find that stars in the outer edges of the Andromeda galaxy are rotating at least as fast as those near the galaxy's center

1970s	Rubin and Ford discover the Rubin-Ford effect early in the decade; late in the decade and in the early 1980s, they show that galaxies are embedded in halos of "dark matter" with a mass five to 10 times greater than that of the visible galaxies
1990s	Early in the decade, Rubin finds a galaxy containing stars that rotate in different directions
1993	Rubin wins National Medal of Science
1996	Rubin becomes first woman since Caroline Herschel to win Royal Astronomical Society's Gold Medal
2002	Rubin wins Gruber International Cosmology Prize
2003	Rubin wins Bruce Medal from Astronomical Society of the Pacific

Further Reading

Books

Lightman, Alan, and Roberta Brawer. *Origins: The Lives and Worlds of Modern Cosmologists.* Cambridge, Mass.: Harvard University Press, 1990.
> Includes a long interview with Rubin.

Rubin, Vera. *Bright Galaxies, Dark Matters.* New York: Springer Verlag, 1996.
> Collection of short essays and talks by Rubin on her work and other astronomical subjects. Includes several biographical interviews.

Yount, Lisa. *Contemporary Women Scientists.* New York: Facts On File, 1994.
> Book for young adults containing a chapter on Rubin that describes her discovery of dark matter and other research.

Articles

Bartusiak, Marcia. "The Woman Who Spins the Stars." *Discover* 11 (October 1990) 88–94.
> Describes Rubin's life and work, focusing on her discovery of dark matter.

Irion, Robert. "The Bright Face behind the Dark Sides of Galaxies." *Science* 295 (February 8, 2002): 960–961.
   Article about Rubin's career that was written when astronomers gave a symposium in her honor.
Rubin, Vera C. "Dark Matter in Spiral Galaxies." *Scientific American* 248 (June 1983): 96–108.
   Description for nonscientists of Rubin's discovery that much of the matter in galaxies gives off no light and is not concentrated in the centers of the galaxies.
———, and W. K. Ford. "Rotation of the Andromeda Nebula from a Spectroscopic Survey of Emission Regions," *Astrophysical Journal* 159 (1970): 379.
   Spectroscopic analysis of the Andromeda galaxy showing that stars in the outer part of the galaxy are orbiting the galaxy's center as fast as, or faster than, stars closer to the center.
———, and others. "Rotation Velocities of 16 Sa Galaxies and a Comparison of Sa, Sb, and Sc Rotation Properties." *Astrophysical Journal* 289 (1985): 81.
   Analysis of rotation speeds of outer and inner material in many kinds of galaxies, confirming that the galaxies must be surrounded by large halos of invisible matter.

9
OTHER STARS, OTHER WORLDS

GEOFFREY MARCY, PAUL BUTLER, AND EXTRASOLAR PLANETS

Paul Butler (left) and Geoffrey Marcy are the world's leading finders of extra-solar planets. Their team of scientists, California & Carnegie Planet Search, has found about two-thirds of the planets so far shown to orbit other stars. (R. Paul Butler, CIW/DTM; Geoffrey W. Marcy, University of California, Berkeley)

While Frank Drake and other SETI researchers scan the heavens for possible signals from civilizations on other planets, other astronomers work on the same problem from the other end: looking for planets from which such signals might come. Although these researchers have not yet located planets likely to harbor life (let alone intelligent life), they have shown that planets in general are far from uncommon. In providing convincing evidence that more than 100 nearby stars have planets, they have begun supplying numbers to fill in Drake's famous equation and have taken the search for extraterrestrial life a step further into the realm of hard science. They have also revised astronomers' ideas about how planetary systems form and what such systems usually look like.

Several astronomical teams are searching for planets orbiting other stars—so-called extrasolar planets, or exoplanets for short—but the kings of planet finding are two American scientists, Geoffrey Marcy and Paul Butler. The team led by Marcy and Butler has found about two-thirds of the total exoplanets discovered so far.

Planet-Hunting Dreams

Like many other scientists, Geoffrey W. Marcy became interested in his chosen field well before he entered college. He was born in 1954 in Detroit, Michigan, but grew up in Southern California. Even as a child, like Frank Drake, Marcy wondered whether other stars had planets and, perhaps, intelligent civilizations.

Marcy's serious study of astronomy began at age 14, when his parents gave him a small telescope. On many nights after that, he got up at 2 A.M., climbed onto his roof, and stared through the telescope at Saturn and Titan, the ringed planet's largest moon. "I was stunned that you could actually see the rings of Saturn," Marcy said in a 2003 interview published on Planetquest, a Web site maintained by the National Aeronautics and Space Administration (NASA) and the California Institute of Technology's Jet Propulsion Laboratory (JPL). "From that moment on, I knew I wanted to be an astronomer."

Marcy majored in both physics and astronomy at the University of California, Los Angeles (UCLA), graduating with the highest honors in 1976. He earned a Ph.D. in astrophysics from the University of

California, Santa Cruz, in 1982, then took postdoctoral training at the Carnegie Institution of Washington's observatories in Pasadena, California, from 1982 to 1984.

Marcy's early research was on magnetic fields in stars, but this subject proved frustrating. Feeling depressed, he realized, as he explained to *Discover* writer Joseph D'Agnese in 2003, that if he was going to remain in astronomy, he needed to "answer questions I relate[d] to on a gut level. I need[ed] to investigate things I cared about as a seven-year-old." At the end of a long shower one day in 1983, he decided that the most compelling of those things was a search for planets outside the solar system. Such a search would certainly be challenging, since no one had yet provided good evidence that extrasolar planets existed.

In 1984, Geoff Marcy became an associate professor of physics and astronomy at San Francisco State University (SFSU) in California. He later advanced to a full professorship. He found few colleagues who shared his hopes for planet-hunting, however—until he met Paul Butler.

An Inspiring Class

R. Paul Butler, born in 1961, grew up in California not far from where Geoff Marcy lived, but they did not know each other at the time. Like Marcy, Butler fell in love with astronomy during his teenage years. Perhaps feeling rebellious, like many teenagers, Butler was excited to learn that the early astronomers Galileo Galilei and Giordano Bruno had been imprisoned and, in Bruno's case, even executed for their ideas. Butler told Joseph D'Agnese that he remembered thinking, "Wow, this is wild, rock-and-roll stuff. The powers that be are *threatened* by it!" Instead of being given a telescope, as Marcy was, Butler built his own.

Butler did not think of looking for extrasolar planets, however, until he took a course from Geoff Marcy at SFSU. Butler had earned a B.A. in physics from the university in 1985, and when he attended Marcy's class in 1986, he was finishing his B.S. in chemistry and, at the same time, starting work on a master's degree in astrophysics. (He completed that degree in 1989 and went on to earn a Ph.D.

in astronomy from the University of Maryland in 1993.) "When Geoff Marcy . . . said to me, 'I think we can find planets around other stars,' " Butler recalled in an article in the spring 1997 *San Francisco State University College of Science & Engineering Alumni Newsletter,* "[I thought] this was one of the most courageous, audacious, visionary, and maybe even insane things I had ever heard. This one sentence changed my life." Butler immediately volunteered to join Marcy's developing planet-search project.

Watching for a Wobble

By the time Paul Butler became Geoff Marcy's planet-hunting partner, other researchers had started to find evidence that extrasolar planets might exist. Astronomers had believed for a long time that planets in the solar system had formed from a disk of dust and gas surrounding the young Sun, and in 1983 and 1984, data from the *Infrared Astronomical Satellite (IRAS)* showed signs of such disks around several nearby stars. More convincing still, astronomers Richard Terrile and Bradford Smith, using a telescope at Las Campanas Observatory in Chile, actually photographed a dust disk around a dwarf star called Beta Pictoris in 1984.

Nonetheless, Marcy and Butler knew that they had no hope of seeing planets, even with the world's best telescopes. The bright light of a star would completely drown out the far weaker glow of even a very large planet. On the other hand, they thought, the same Doppler shifting of starlight that had shown Edwin Hubble the expanding universe and revealed the motion of distant stars to Vera Rubin might offer a way to detect planets indirectly.

A star, of course, is far more massive than even the largest planets that might circle it. The star's gravity, therefore, will pull powerfully on its planets. Indeed, planets' orbits are determined by a balance between the star's gravity, which draws the planets toward the star, and the planets' forward motion, which flings them away.

Gravity, however, is a two-way street. Planets have their own mass, so their gravity tugs on their stars as well as vice versa. Although much weaker than that of the star, the gravity of a large planet could pull on a star enough to make the star sway or wobble slightly as the planet goes around it. As the star moved a little closer to Earth, Marcy and Butler realized, the star's motion would show in a slight shifting of its light toward the blue end of the spectrum. As the star wobbled in the other direction, its light would be pushed toward the red. The extent of the shifts could reveal the planet's minimum mass. The time period required for a cycle of changes would show how long the planet took to orbit its star.

The idea that planets could cause Doppler shifts in starlight was not hard to understand, but finding a way to observe such changes was daunting. Marcy and Butler knew that the shifts would be extremely small, so detecting them would require both very sharp spectrograms (images of spectra) and powerful computers to analyze the photos. Butler spent the late 1980s and early 1990s developing new software and other technology that would let him detect tinier Doppler changes than had ever been possible before. Meanwhile, starting in spring 1987, he and Marcy obtained spectrograms of 120 Sun-like stars within 100 light-years of Earth with a telescope and spectrograph at Lick Observatory in San Jose, a short drive from SFSU.

After Lick's spectrograph was improved in November 1994, Butler and Marcy became able to measure changes in a star's movement as small as 10 feet (3 m) a second, about the speed of a person walking quickly. Even so, they could not find convincing evidence of a single planet.

The First Exoplanets

In October 1995, Marcy and Butler were dumbfounded to learn that two Swiss astronomers had succeeded where they had failed. Michel Mayor and Didier Queloz of the Geneva Observatory reported that they had found Doppler shifts in the spectrum of a Sun-like star called 51 Pegasi, about 45 light-years from Earth, in the constellation of Pegasus (the winged horse). The changes suggested that a planet about the size of Jupiter orbited very close to the star, passing around it once every 4.2 days.

Not surprisingly, Butler and Marcy had mixed feelings about the Swiss team's discovery. "On the one hand," Marcy told *Time* reporter Michael Lemonick, "[I was disappointed that] we had been scooped. But I also felt euphoric that humanity had entered a new era in which new worlds were going to be subject to exploration." He and Butler hurried back to their computers, first to confirm the Swiss team's finding and then to reexamine their own data, looking for wobbles with very short time cycles.

On December 30, 1995, Paul Butler, working at the scientists' office in Berkeley, saw his computer produce a graph showing that 70 Virginis, a star in the constellation of Virgo (the Virgin), had the kind of wobble that indicated the presence of a planet. "When I saw the data come up, I was completely blown away," Butler said to Michael Lemonick. "It knocked me off my chair."

Marcy, for his part, recalled in his Planetquest interview, "I was at home, preparing for New Year's Eve. . . . Paul Butler called me up and said . . . 'Geoff, come here.' here." . . . I drove immediately to Berkeley. . . . We had been looking for planets around stars for eleven years without a single success, and there on the computer screen was the first planet we had ever discovered. It was a fantastic moment."

A String of Spectacular Finds

Butler and Marcy announced their discovery of 70 Virginis and another planet-bearing star, 47 Ursae Majoris (in the Great Bear, or Big Dipper), in January 1996. As the number of reported exoplanets grew in the years that followed, Butler and Marcy continued to find more of these planets than anyone else. Their software gave them an advantage in analyzing information, and their early years of collecting provided a tremendous amount of data with which to work. They added to that data with a new survey of 400 stars, using the 33-foot (10-m) Keck Telescope in Hawaii, which began in July 1996.

In March 1999, Butler and Marcy located the first star system shown to have multiple planets. They reported that three huge planets circle Upsilon Andromedae, a star in the constellation Andromeda. The innermost planet has a circular orbit, while the two outer ones follow egg-shaped paths. By 2002, Marcy and Butler had found three other multiple-planet systems.

Although most astronomers accepted the idea that stars' tiny Doppler "wobbles" were caused by the gravitational tug of planets, a few thought that the shifts might result from changes within the stars instead. Marcy and Butler's team disposed of that objection by showing the existence of an extrasolar planet in a different way in 1999. Marcy found evidence that the star HD 209458 had a very large planet with an orbit that would make the planet transit the star,

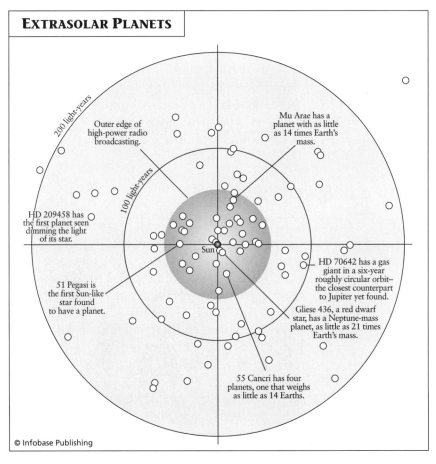

EXTRASOLAR PLANETS

200 light-years

100 light-years

Outer edge of high-power radio broadcasting.

Mu Arae has a planet with as little as 14 times Earth's mass.

HD 209458 has the first planet seen dimming the light of its star.

Sun

51 Pegasi is the first Sun-like star found to have a planet.

HD 70642 has a gas giant in a six-year roughly circular orbit– the closest counterpart to Jupiter yet found.

Gliese 436, a red dwarf star, has a Neptune-mass planet, as little as 21 times Earth's mass.

55 Cancri has four planets, one that weighs as little as 14 Earths.

© Infobase Publishing

This map, with the solar system at its center, shows the location of some of the approximately 140 extrasolar planets found so far.

TRENDS: DISCOVERY OF EXTRASOLAR PLANETS

As the number of known extrasolar planets has grown, Geoffrey Marcy and Paul Butler have kept their place as the leading planet finders. The following table shows how the total number of planets and the total discovered by Marcy and Butler's team, the California and Carnegie Planet Search, have changed over time.

Year	Total planets discovered	Number found by Marcy-Butler team
1996	7	6
1999	29	19
2001	78	45
2003	96	65
2005	136	100

---

or pass directly between the star and Earth. When the transit took place, he pointed out, the planet should block a little of the star's light and therefore slightly decrease the star's brightness. On November 7, Greg Henry, a member of Marcy's team, found a 1.7 percent drop in HD 209458's brightness at exactly the time Marcy had predicted that the planet would pass in front of the star. Since then, several other exoplanets have been shown to transit their stars.

Strange Worlds

Although planets have been found around only 10 percent of the Sun-like stars inspected so far, most experts in the field think that many, if not most, Sun-like stars will turn out to have planetary systems when astronomers become able to detect smaller planets. "It looks like planet formation is a normal process," University of Arizona planetary scientist Jonathan Lunine said in a December 2004 *National Geographic* article. Most planetary systems, however, seem to be very different from the one in which Earth resides.

For one thing, almost all the extrasolar planets reported to date appear to be the size of Jupiter or larger. This is partly because the wobbles produced by small planets are still very hard to detect. The smallest planet found so far, located by Marcy's team in June 2005, is 7.5 times the size of Earth.

Astronomers have been startled to learn that most planets found so far seem to orbit very close to their stars, far closer than Mercury is to the Sun. The planets circle the stars in as little as three days. Because these planets practically graze their stars, the planets' surface temperature is very high. They have therefore been nicknamed "hot Jupiters" or "roasters." Cooler planets with more distant orbits may be detected as observations continue, however.

Some planets have given astronomers a second surprise. Most experts thought that extrasolar planets would have more or less circular orbits, as the planets in the solar system do. Many planets around other stars, however, possess oval, or eccentric, orbits.

So far, extrasolar planets seem unlikely to carry living things. Like Jupiter and the other large outer planets in the solar system, these planets are probably made of gas rather than rock. Because most orbit so close to their stars, they are far too hot to sustain life as earthly scientists understand it. A few planets, however, appear to be small and cool enough to contain liquid water, a necessity for life on Earth. Geoff Marcy thinks that as planet-hunting technology improves, more small, rocky, water-bearing planets will be found. One group of scientists calculated in 2005 that up to half of star systems with planets will include planets that can support life.

Future Planet Hunts

Many groups of scientists continue to discover new extrasolar planets and learn more about those already known. In 2001, for instance, astronomers using the *Hubble Space Telescope* directly detected the atmosphere of an extrasolar planet for the first time. The planet was a gas giant orbiting the star HD209458, the same star whose dimming light gave Marcy and Butler their first look at a transiting extrasolar planet in 1999.

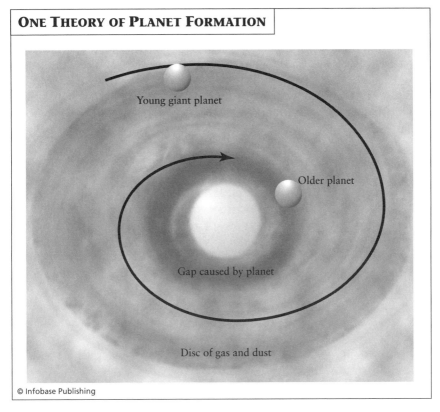

ONE THEORY OF PLANET FORMATION

Young giant planet

Older planet

Gap caused by planet

Disc of gas and dust

© Infobase Publishing

According to one theory of planet formation, large planets take shape far away from their parent stars, in the thickest part of the disks of dust and gas that surround many young stars. As such a planet scoops up nearby matter, it forms a gap in the disk. Friction between gas molecules and solid particles eventually slows down the disk's rotation, and the star's gravity begins to pull material from the disk closer to the star. As the material spirals inward, it brings the gap and the planet with it. In time, the planet settles into a stable orbit very close to the star.

CONNECTIONS: HOW PLANETS FORM

Planet-hunting research has completely changed astronomers' ideas about the way planetary systems develop. Researchers believed that planets formed only from the middle part of disks of dust and gas spinning around young stars, like the disk seen around Beta Pictoris. Material near the outer or inner edge of the disk, they thought, would be too thin to clump together into planets. By orbiting so close to their stars, however, many extrasolar planets seem to challenge that theory. Some astronomers think that some of these planets formed farther from the stars and then spiraled inward, eventually settling into short, stable orbits.

Traditional views of planet system formation also have trouble explaining extrasolar planets' eccentric orbits. One possibility is that when several large planets go around the same star, the planets tug on each other enough to give their orbits an oval shape. A secondary star, so far invisible, might also distort the planets' orbits. Alternatively, planets in a newly formed system might collide like balls on a pool table, changing their orbits abruptly.

Among other things, research on exoplanets suggests that Earth may owe its existence to Jupiter—or rather to the fact that Jupiter has a stable, more or less circular orbit. If the giant planet had had a more oval orbit, it might have shattered Earth or knocked the smaller planet out of the solar system. University of Arizona astronomer Jonathan Lunine thinks Jupiter may have helped Earth in a second way as well, by pulling on the small, rocky bodies that formed in the dust disk around the young Sun. The pull would have distorted the rocks' orbits, making them likely to collide with each other. Collisions of many such Moon-size clumps of rock would be necessary to build up a planet the size of Earth.

Scientists using the *Spitzer Space Telescope* (named for Lyman Spitzer, Jr., the "father" of the *Hubble Space Telescope*), an observatory satellite that detects infrared radiation, described further studies of this planet, as well as a second one orbiting a star in the constellation Lyra, in March 2005. The *Spitzer* picked up the infrared glow from the planets, which are thought to have a temperature of about 1,340°F (727°C). Potentially, infrared information can tell astronomers what chemicals a planet's atmosphere contains. In the same month, other scientists using the European Southern Observatory's Very Large Telescope in Chile, one of Riccardo Giacconi's projects, took an optical photograph of a planet orbiting a young star, GQ Lupi.

Plans are also being made for even better planet hunting, both on Earth and in space. For example, some new ground-based telescopes, such as the Large Binocular Telescope on Mount Graham in Arizona, will use a process called nulling interferometry to hunt for planets. The twin mirrors of the telescope will let astronomers essentially cancel out the bright light of a star, allowing planets near the star to be seen.

NASA has big plans for planet finding too. In 1996, soon after Butler, Marcy, and others began reporting extrasolar planets, NASA administrator Daniel S. Goldin announced the establishment of what he called the Origins Project, which would consist of several space telescopes specifically designed to hunt for such planets.

The first telescope, called *Kepler* (for Johannes Kepler, the German astronomer who worked out the orbits of planets in the solar system in the early 17th century), is scheduled to be launched in 2008. Using a specialized telescope called a photometer, it will detect extrasolar planets that transit their stars by using very sensitive charge-coupled devices to measure the small changes in brightness that the transits cause. *Kepler* will scan thousands of stars over a four-year period and is expected to be able to "see" planets as small as Earth.

SIM PlanetQuest, on which Marcy is a principal investigator, may launch around 2011 if budgetary concerns are resolved. Consisting of a set of small telescopes that work together to make single images, it will conduct both a "deep search," in which it looks carefully for planets around about 250 nearby stars, and a "broad survey," in which it will make less detailed scans of about 2,000 stars.

The most ambitious part of the Origins Project, the *Terrestrial Planet Finder (TPF),* has two parts. One is a coronagraph, which blocks out the central light of a star (much as an eclipse does) so that the star's outer edges and any nearby planets can be photographed.

The other is a nulling interferometer working at infrared wavelengths. NASA hopes to launch the coronagraph around 2014 and the interferometer before 2020 if Congress reverses its postponing of the project. When fully assembled, *TPF* is expected to be able to pick up light from exoplanets the size of Earth and analyze it to determine what materials are in the planet's atmosphere and, perhaps, even on its surface.

Looking for a New Home

Wherever planet hunting leads, Geoff Marcy and Paul Butler plan to go. The two scientists still work together, even though their "home bases" are now across the country from each other. After holding the position of Distinguished University Professor at San Francisco State between 1997 and 1999, Marcy moved to the University of California, Berkeley, becoming a professor of astronomy there. He also became the director of the university's new Center for Integrative Planetary Science, a group of biologists, chemists, astronomers, and physicists working together to look for life outside the solar system. In 1999, the same year Marcy moved to Berkeley, Butler joined Vera Rubin and other astronomers at the Carnegie Institution of Washington's Department of Terrestrial Magnetism.

Today Butler and Marcy lead a team that continues the extensive project they began in the mid-1990s. Besides studying 1,000 Northern Hemisphere stars at the Lick and Keck Observatories, the project now observes the brightest Southern Hemisphere stars with the Anglo-Australian telescope in New South Wales, Australia, and the Carnegie Institution's Magellan telescopes in Chile. This project, expected to be completed by 2010, will examine all 2,000 Sun-like stars within 150 light-years of the solar system.

Marcy and Butler have already received considerable publicity, including a *Time* magazine cover story in 1996, and many honors for their research on extrasolar planets. Prizes they have shared include the Bioastronomy Medal of the International Astronomical Union (1997), the Henry Draper Medal of the National Academy of Sciences (2001), the Carl Sagan Award from the American Astronautical Society and the Planetary Society (2002), and the Beatrice Tinsley Prize of the American Astronomical Society (2002).

Both men find the thrill of spotting new planets more important than any award, however. Geoff Marcy's wife, chemist Susan Kegley, told Salon.com writer William Speed Weed in 1999 that Marcy "has kept that childlike wonder of his science—the curiosity that put him on the roof at the age of 14 with his little telescope," and the same is surely true of Paul Butler.

Marcy also hopes that, by hunting faraway worlds, he is ultimately doing something important for Earth. Unlike Frank Drake, he believes that humans will someday colonize planets around other stars. Marcy told *Discover* magazine's Joseph D'Agnese, "If we diversify cosmically, our presence is more secure. We're vulnerable being on one rock. I think what Paul and I are doing is finding ports of call where we can go someday and, in a sense, drop anchor."

Chronology

1954	Geoffrey W. Marcy born in Detroit, Michigan
1961	Paul Butler born in California
1976	Marcy earns B.S. from University of California, Los Angeles
1982	Marcy earns Ph.D. in astrophysics from University of California, Santa Cruz
1983	Marcy changes research specialty to search for extrasolar planets
1984	Marcy becomes associate professor of physics and astronomy at San Francisco State University (SFSU); Infrared Astronomical Satellite (IRAS) shows evidence of dust disks around several stars; Richard Terrile and Bradford Smith photograph a disk of possible planet-forming material around the star Beta Pictoris
1985	Paul Butler earns B.A. in physics from SFSU
1986	Butler takes class from Geoff Marcy, who interests him in looking for extrasolar planets; Butler earns a B.S. in chemistry from SFSU

1987	Butler and Marcy begin photographing spectra of nearby stars at Lick Observatory
1989	Butler completes master's degree in astrophysics at SFSU
1993	Butler earns Ph.D. in astronomy from University of Maryland
1994	In November, improvements in equipment at Lick Observatory allow Butler and Marcy to detect changes in a star's movement as small as 10 feet (3 m) per second
1995	Michel Mayor and Didier Queloz report discovery of the first extrasolar planet in October; on December 30, Marcy and Butler find evidence of a second planet, orbiting the star 70 Virginis, in their own computer data
1996	Butler and Marcy announce discovery of planets orbiting 70 Virginis and 47 Ursae Majoris in January; in July, Marcy and Butler begin observing stars with the Keck Telescope
1997	Marcy becomes Distinguished University Professor at SFSU
1999	Marcy becomes professor of astronomy and director of the Center for Integrative Planetary Science at the University of California, Berkeley; Butler joins staff of the Carnegie Institution of Washington's Department of Terrestrial Magnetism in Washington, D.C.; in March, Marcy and Butler discover Upsilon Andromedae, the first star shown to have multiple planets; on November 7 they show that a planet transiting the star HD 209458 causes the light of that star to dim
2001	Marcy and Butler win Henry Draper medal from National Academy of Sciences; astronomers using *Hubble Space Telescope* directly detect atmosphere of extrasolar planet
2002	Butler and Marcy win Beatrice Tinsley Prize from American Astronomical Society
2005	In March, two teams use *Spitzer Space Telescope* to see infrared glow of two extrasolar planets; other astronomers using the Very Large Telescope in Chile photograph an extrasolar planet orbiting the star GQ Lupi; in June, Marcy's group finds a planet 7.5 times the size of Earth, the smallest discovered so far.

Further Reading

Books

Anton, Ted. *Bold Science: Seven Scientists Who Are Changing Our World.* New York: W. H. Freeman, 2000.
> Includes a chapter on Marcy.

Bartusiak, Marcia, ed. *Archives of the Universe: A Treasury of Astronomy's Historic Works of Discovery.* New York: Pantheon Books, 2004.
> Includes papers describing early discoveries of extrasolar planets by Mayor and Queloz and by Butler and Marcy.

Articles

Appenzeller, Tim. "Search for Other Earths." *National Geographic* 206 (December 2004): 68–95.
> Well-illustrated article describes types of extrasolar planets detected so far, methods of detection, and future extended planet searches, including some that will use telescopes in space.

Butler, R. Paul. "Extrasolar Planets: First Reconnaissance." American Association of Amateur Astronomers Web site. Available online. URL: http://www.astromax.org/adastra2002/butlerpg.htm. Accessed on January 31, 2005.
> Talk given by Butler to the association in 2002 describes some characteristics of the first extrasolar planets to be discovered and tells what they suggest about the way planets form.

D'Agnese, Joseph. "Geoff Marcy and Paul Butler: The Astronomers Who Proved Carl Sagan Correct." *Discover* 24 (November 2003): 40–42.
> Brief description of Marcy, Butler, and their discoveries of extrasolar planets.

Lemonick, Michael D. "Searching for Other Worlds." *Time* 147 (February 5, 1996): 52–57.
> Cover story focusing on the work of Butler and Marcy, written soon after the discovery of the first extrasolar planets.

Marcy, Geoffrey W., and R. Paul Butler. "Giant Planets Orbiting Faraway Stars." *Scientific American* 278 (March 1998).
> Describes technique used to discover first extrasolar planets, characteristics of the planets, implications for theories about how planets form, and the future of planet hunting.

Planetquest. "Leading Planet-Finder Predicts Discovery of Another 'Earth' Within Decade." California Institute of Technology Jet Propulsion Laboratory and NASA Web site. Available online. URL: http://planetquest.jpl.nasa.gov/news/marcy.html. Posted on April 7, 2003. Accessed on January 31, 2005.

> Interview with Geoffrey Marcy.

SFSU.edu. "Planet Hunter: R. Paul Butler." *San Francisco State College of Science & Engineering Alumni Newsletter,* spring 1997. Available online. URL: http://www.sfsu.edu/~science/newsletters/spring1997/alumnidomain.html. Accessed on January 31, 2005.

> Brief description of Paul Butler's career to 1997.

Weed, William Speed. "Master of the Universe." Salon.com. Available online. URL: http://archive.salon.com/people/feature/1999/12/02/marcy. Posted on December 2, 1999. Accessed on January 31, 2005.

> Extensive profile of Geoffrey Marcy.

Web Sites

California & Carnegie Planet Search. URL: http://exoplanets.org. Accessed on March 31, 2005.

> This is the Web site of Marcy and Butler's planet-finding group, cosponsored by the University of California and the Carnegie Institution of Washington and supported by NASA, the National Science Foundation, and Sun Microsystems. The site includes news about the group's latest discoveries, a list of all extrasolar planets found so far, types of planets found, descriptions of planet detection techniques, and additional resources (articles, books, and Web sites).

Origins Project. URL: http://origins.jpl.nasa.gov. Accessed on September 26, 2005.

> This site describes the components of the Origins Project, a joint effort of NASA and the California Institute of Technology's Jet Propulsion Laboratory to look for extrasolar planets. The project includes the proposed space telescopes *Kepler, SIM PlanetQuest,* and *Terrestrial Planet Finder.* In addition to describing the spacecraft and their missions, the site provides news about the project and related information.

10
A "CREEPY" END?

SAUL PERLMUTTER, BRIAN SCHMIDT, AND
DARK ENERGY

In 1931, an astronomer's discovery convinced one of the most respected scientists of all time that he—along with earlier astronomers—had been wrong. Albert Einstein had added a term, the *cosmological constant,* to the equations defining his general theory of relativity in 1917 because astronomers of that era told him that the size of the universe did not change over time. To make his equations show such a universe, Einstein decided he needed a factor that opposes gravity by pushing matter and space apart. The cosmological constant stood for this factor. However, when Edwin Hubble proved that the universe was expanding, a possibility predicted in the original relativity equations, Einstein concluded that the constant was not necessary. According to an often-told story, the renowned physicist thanked Hubble for saving him from "the greatest blunder of my life."

If Einstein had been alive in 1998, astronomy might have made him change his mind again. In that year, competing international groups of astronomers led by Saul Perlmutter and Brian Schmidt showed that the force represented by the cosmological constant may exist after all. Using a new way of measuring distance to faraway galaxies, the two teams came to a startling conclusion: The universe is not only expanding but speeding up. Furthermore, just as Vera Rubin showed that the amount of dark matter dwarfs the amount of familiar, visible matter, these researchers say that matter of all kinds is outweighed by something more mysterious still—a force within empty space itself, called dark energy.

Exploding "Candles"

The explosive idea of dark energy, which has upended astronomy and physics, grew out of a study of exploding stars—supernovas. Astronomers can identify two main types of supernovas, Ia and II, by looking at their spectra. In the late 1980s, scientists noticed that

Saul Perlmutter of Lawrence Berkeley National Laboratory heads the Supernova Cosmology Project, one of two teams whose observation of distant supernovas showed in 1998 that an unknown force called dark energy opposes and outweighs the effects of all the gravity in the universe. Dark energy is speeding up the rate at which the universe is expanding. Perlmutter is seated in front of a picture of the Tarantula Nebula. The bright star to the right of Perlmutter's ladder is Supernova 1987a, a type II supernova. (Lawrence Berkeley National Laboratory)

the spectra of type II supernovas varied quite a bit, but the spectra for most type Ia supernovas looked almost exactly alike. The supernovas' brightness at their most intense also was about the same. This meant that these stellar fireworks displays, like the Cepheid stars Edwin Hubble had used to find out how far away the Andromeda galaxy was, might provide a way to measure distances in the universe. The supernovas, however, could make much longer yardsticks than Cepheids

---

I WAS THERE: A NEW STAR

In their anthology of historical descriptions of supernovas, David H. Clark and F. Richard Stephenson quote a translation of Danish astronomer Tycho Brahe's account of a supernova he saw in 1572. This star was the most recent type Ia supernova seen in the Milky Way galaxy.

On [November 11, 1572] a little before dinner . . . during my walk contemplating the sky . . . behold, directly overhead a certain strange star was suddenly seen, flashing its light with a radiant gleam and it struck my eyes. Amazed, and as if astonished and stupefied, I stood still, gazing for a certain length of time with my eyes fixed intently on it and noticing that same star placed close to the stars which antiquity attributed to [the constellation] Cassiopeia. When I had satisfied myself that no star of that kind had ever shone forth before, I was led into such perplexity by the unbelievability of the thing that I began to doubt the faith of my own eyes, and so, turning to the servants who were accompanying me, I asked them whether they too could see [it]. . . . They immediately replied with one voice that they saw it completely and that it was extremely bright. . . . Still being doubtful on account of the novelty of the thing, I enquired of some country people who by chance were traveling past in carriages whether they could see a certain star in the height. Indeed these people shouted out that they saw that huge star, which had never been noticed so high up. And at length . . . I began to measure its situation [location] and distance from the neighboring stars . . . and to note . . . those things which were visible to the eye concerning its apparent size, form, color, and other aspects.

because the supernovas can be seen from much farther away. A type Ia supernova at its brightest can outshine a whole galaxy.

Having dependable landmarks—or "standard candles," as astronomers call them—that work over such great distances could let cosmologists answer some very important questions. Because light takes time to travel, *far away* in astronomy also means *long ago:* The most distant galaxies are also the oldest. Edwin Hubble's description of the expanding universe said that these galaxies are also moving the fastest, so their spectra show the greatest Doppler shifts toward the red. If type Ia supernovas proved to be accurate standard candles, astronomers could compare the distance figures obtained by measuring the apparent brightness of the supernovas with those determined by measuring the size of their redshifts. The comparison would show whether the rate at which the universe was expanding had changed over time. By comparing information about faraway galaxies with predictions made by Einstein's relativity theory, astronomers could also find out how much matter the universe contains, the shape of space, and even how the universe will end.

Before astronomers could use type Ia supernovas as standard candles, however, they had to show that the supernovas were as alike as studies of a few nearby ones had suggested. To do so, researchers would have to examine the spectra of many more supernovas, including distant ones. Near the end of the 1980s, a group of astronomers centered in California began trying to do just that.

The Supernova Cosmology Project

The California group had its headquarters at Lawrence Berkeley National Laboratory (LBL), which the University of California, Berkeley (UC Berkeley), manages for the U.S. Department of Energy. The laboratory, named after famed physicist E. O. Lawrence, had long been famous as a center for high-energy physics, but in the 1970s, it also began doing research in astrophysics.

In the early 1980s, Richard Muller, a physics professor at UC Berkeley and an astrophysicist at LBL, led a project to develop the first robotic telescope, which could steer itself and analyze its observations automatically. This automation sped up boring astronomical tasks, especially that of looking for supernovas. One of the graduate students whom Muller interested in his automated telescope was a young man from Philadelphia named Saul Perlmutter.

Perlmutter, born in 1959 in Champaign-Urbana, Illinois (his family moved to Pennsylvania when he was about four years old), came to Berkeley to study subatomic physics. He had majored in physics at Harvard, from which he graduated in 1981 with the highest honors. Nonetheless, soon after Perlmutter arrived in California in 1983, he changed his focus to astrophysics because research in that field did not require the large groups of people and expensive machines that had come to dominate high-energy physics. Perlmutter preferred working with smaller, more intimate teams.

While doing research at LBL as a graduate student, Perlmutter became part of the Berkeley Automatic Supernova Search Team, a newly established group trying to find out whether supernovas could be used as standard candles. The team looked at type II supernovas first, but these proved to have too many differences in their spectra and brightness to be dependable yardsticks, so the group soon turned to studying type Ia supernovas. Perlmutter obtained his Ph.D. in 1986 with a thesis on techniques for using the robotic telescope to look for supernovas, then continued at LBL as a postdoctoral fellow.

In 1988, Perlmutter and another postdoctoral student, Carl Pennypacker, formed a new research group to look for supernovas with high redshifts—in other words, very distant ones, billions rather than millions of light-years away. At the time, most astronomers doubted whether such supernovas could be found in any quantity, but Perlmutter believed that a combination of wide-angle cameras, new software, and larger telescopes could accomplish it. The two called their group the Supernova Cosmology Project (SCP) to reflect their hope that supernovas could be used to answer fundamental questions about the universe, such as whether the speed of its expansion had changed over time. Working with British astronomers using the 13-foot (4-m) Isaac Newton Telescope in the Canary Islands, the SCP found its first high-redshift supernova in spring 1992.

Saul Perlmutter became the SCP's sole leader around 1989, when Pennypacker's interests turned elsewhere. Harvard astronomy professor Robert Kirshner wrote in *The Extravagant Universe* that Perlmutter was an excellent choice for the group's head because Perlmutter "was very determined, had good judgment about what was most important, and made a forceful spokesman for the project."

The High-Z Supernova Search Team

The Supernova Cosmology Project was not the only group that wanted to measure the universe with supernovas. Robert Kirshner at Harvard, for one, had been studying these explosive stars since his own college days in the late 1960s. In the early 1990s, as the Berkeley group had done earlier, Kirshner's team tried using type II supernovas as standard candles, but around 1993 they, too, turned to type Ia supernovas.

Brian Schmidt, one of Kirshner's graduate students, came to share Kirshner's fascination with supernovas. Schmidt was used to seeing the stars above wide, open spaces. Born in 1967 in Montana, he had grown up in that state's "big sky country" and, later, under the shimmering auroras of Alaska. His father, a biologist, taught him to love nature and science, and Schmidt decided at an early age that he, too, would become a scientist. His sixth-grade teacher was so impressed with his knowledge of astronomy that she asked him to teach the astronomy unit of her science class.

Brian Schmidt of Australian National Universities' Research School of Astronomy and Astrophysics leads the High-Z Supernova Search Team, the group that sometimes competed and sometimes cooperated with Saul Perlmutter's team to discover type Ia supernovas and use them to find out the structure and fate of the universe. (Australian National Universities)

A highly respected astronomy department drew Schmidt to the

University of Arizona. He graduated with B.S. degrees in both astronomy and physics in 1989, then went to Harvard to study for his doctorate under Kirshner. Schmidt earned his Ph.D. in astronomy in 1993 with a thesis on type II supernovas and continued working with Kirshner for postdoctoral studies.

In 1994, Kirshner and Schmidt established their own international group to look for distant type Ia supernovas, which they called the High-Z Supernova Search Team. (Astronomers use Z to represent the value of an object's redshift; the higher the value of Z, the greater

---

OTHER SCIENTISTS: ROBERT KIRSHNER

Born in Long Branch, New Jersey, on August 15, 1949, Robert Kirshner first became involved with supernovas when he did a project on the Crab Nebula during his junior year at Harvard University. The Crab Nebula is the remains of a supernova that was visible from Earth in A.D. 1054 His interest in astronomy stirred, Kirshner went on to make ultraviolet observations of the Sun in his senior year, and his thesis on that project won the university's Bowdoin Prize for "useful and polite literature." He graduated from Harvard in 1970.

Remembering his Crab Nebula project fondly, Kirshner returned to supernova research for his Ph.D. work at the California Institute of Technology (Caltech). He started thinking about the possible use of type I supernovas as standard candles when he sorted supernova spectra and noticed how much alike the spectra of type I supernovas were. He earned his doctorate in astronomy in 1975.

After postdoctoral work at Kitt Peak National Observatory in Arizona, Kirshner joined the faculty of the University of Michigan in 1977. He returned to Harvard and the Harvard-Smithsonian Center for Astrophysics in 1985. He headed the Harvard astronomy department from 1990 to 1997 and was associate director for optical and infrared astronomy at the Harvard-Smithsonian center from 1998 to 2003. In 1994, he inspired the creation of the High-Z Supernova Search Team, one of the two groups studying type Ia supernovas with large redshifts. He is currently Clowes Professor of Science and professor of astronomy at Harvard.

SOLVING PROBLEMS: BATCH PROCESSING

The Berkeley and Harvard teams used similar methods to find their supernovas, drawing on technology pioneered largely by Perlmutter's group. They combined large, sensitive charge-coupled devices (CCDs)—essentially digital cameras for astronomy—with telescopes that covered a large patch of sky in a single image. Using this combination, they made two images of the same area several weeks apart, then used sophisticated computer software to compare them.

Dots of light that appeared on one image but not on the other might be supernovas. On the other hand, the dots might also represent artificial satellites or other unimportant objects. Only a larger telescope could tell for sure. The groups therefore faced what Saul Perlmutter, in a 2002 Lawrence Berkeley National Laboratory press release, called a "chicken-and-egg problem": They needed large telescopes to determine the identity of their mystery spots and obtain spectra if the objects did prove to be supernovas, but at the same time, they had to have dependable crops of supernova candidates in hand before they could obtain observing time on such telescopes.

The Supernova Cosmology Project used what Perlmutter termed *batch processing* to solve this problem. "The key was to clump the observations," he said in the 2002 press release. His team made its first wide-angle image just after the new Moon, when the night sky was very dark, and the second image three weeks later, when the Moon was waning. Their software could compare the two images, each containing thousands of galaxies, in only a few hours and pinpoint one or two dozen probable supernovas in each batch. That was enough to persuade allocation committees to grant the group observing time on telescopes such as Hawaii's Keck. The team then still had at least a week of dark skies to obtain spectra and measurements of brightness for their most likely candidates, using the big telescopes.

The Berkeley group demonstrated the reliability of batch processing by 1994. When the High-Z team formed, it adopted a similar technique. By 1996, both groups were finding distant supernovas every month.

the redshift and the farther away the object is.) Schmidt, an expert in search software like Perlmutter, became head of the team in 1995, just about the time he moved to Australia with his Australian-born wife, Jenny, and began working at the Mount Stromlo and Siding Spring Observatories, located just outside of Canberra. The observatories are now known as the Australian National Universities' Research School of Astronomy and Astrophysics, and Schmidt is now an Australian Research Council Professor there.

Big Questions

By 1996, researchers had found ways to compensate for small differences in type Ia spectra. The astronomical community became convinced that, with these adjustments, type Ia supernovas were dependable "candles" for determining distances to far-flung galaxies. For both the Supernova Cosmology Project and the High-Z Supernova Search Team, the race was on to find and analyze as many distant (high-redshift) supernovas as they could. The more supernovas they checked, the more accurate the conclusions based on their measurements would be.

The first thing the two search groups wanted their supernovas to tell them was whether, and how, the speed at which the universe was expanding had changed over time. They could determine this by comparing the supernovas' distance as calculated from their redshifts with their distance as calculated from their apparent brightness. If supernovas with large redshifts proved to be brighter (and therefore closer to Earth) than their redshifts said they should be, this would mean that the universe was expanding faster in the distant past, when light left the supernovas, than it is now. In other words, the pull of gravity would be slowing down the expansion rate. If the supernovas were fainter than expected, on the other hand, the expansion rate would be speeding up. If the results of the two methods matched, the rate had stayed the same.

The change in expansion rate, in turn, could let cosmologists essentially weigh the universe. The more mass the cosmos contains, the greater the effect gravity should have on the universe's expansion. Most astronomers expected the universe to contain enough mass for gravity to slow the rate of expansion, just as the pull of Earth's gravity slows down and eventually reverses the movement of a ball thrown into the air. Their main question was how great the slowing down would be.

The amount of mass in the universe determines how the universe will end. If the amount of mass is great enough to make the rate of expansion slow considerably, gravity eventually will overcome the repulsive force of the big bang and begin pulling matter and space back together again. All the galaxies will finally crush down into an infinitesimally tiny point, producing a big crunch, or, as Robert Kirshner and his group like to call it, a "gnab gib"—"big bang" backward.

If the universe has less mass, gravity and the repulsive force of the big bang might balance exactly, or the repulsive force might be stronger than gravity. In these cases, the universe will go on expanding forever.

Astounding Conclusions

Toward the end of 1997, both supernova groups looked at their results and could hardly believe what they saw. (According to Robert Kirshner's book, Brian Schmidt said he viewed his figures with "somewhere between amazement and horror.") The distant supernovas the teams had studied were fainter than their redshifts said they should be—were 25 percent fainter, in fact, than they should have been if the cosmos contained no matter at all. In other words, instead of slowing down or even staying the same, the rate at which the universe was expanding seemed to be speeding up.

The teams rechecked their calculations and feverishly gathered more supernovas, trying to remove possible causes of mistakes, but they found nothing that changed their results. They had to face the startling conclusion that something besides matter and gravity was affecting the way the universe behaves. This "antigravity" force had to be far stronger than leftover energy from the big bang. The only such force that anyone could think of was the one represented by the cosmological constant, which Albert Einstein had figuratively thrown in his wastebasket in 1931.

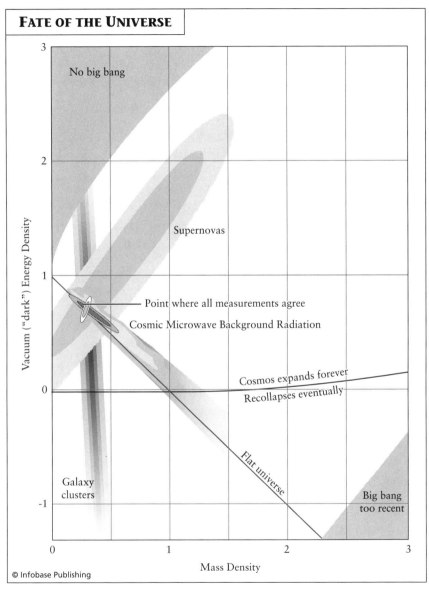

FATE OF THE UNIVERSE

Data from supernovas, the cosmic microwave background radiation, and galaxy clusters all agree that the total density of the universe is 1, meaning that space is flat and the universe will continue expanding forever. Mass affected by gravity makes up about 30 percent of the total, and dark, or vacuum, energy, which opposes gravity, comprises the rest.

The competing groups were torn between wanting to be the first to announce this amazing discovery and fearing to be proven wrong. Both presented some of their supernova calculations at a meeting of the American Astronomical Society in January 1998, and Alex Filippenko discussed the High-Z group's results further at a second scientific meeting in February. Each group stressed a different aspect of their research: Perlmutter talked about the cosmological constant and a possible new form of energy, whereas Filippenko focused on the accelerating universe. The High-Z team published its results in the September 1998 *Astronomical Journal,* and the SCP had its paper in the June 1, 1999, *Astrophysical Journal.*

Although the two groups have sometimes argued about which should receive more credit for their discovery, they say that the fact that both reached the same conclusion is far more important. They studied different supernovas and analyzed the supernovas' spectra in different ways. Nonetheless, as Perlmutter put it in a 1998 LBL press release, their results ultimately were in "remarkably violent agreement."

New Picture of the Universe

The prestigious magazine *Science* called the supernova teams' discovery the "breakthrough of the year" for 1998—and no wonder. The proposed existence of what soon came to be called dark energy turned cosmology and physics upside down.

Other scientists had trouble believing the groups' claims at first, but the two teams' similar figures helped to convince doubters that the supernova searchers had found a phenomenon as real as it was amazing. Since 1998, furthermore, many of the supernova groups' conclusions about the nature of the universe have been supported by results that other researchers obtained in completely different ways.

The most important confirmation has come from studies of the cosmic background radiation. The most dramatic measurements of this radiation came from two NASA satellites, the *Cosmic Background Explorer (COBE,* launched in 1989) and the *Wilkinson Microwave Anisotropy Probe (WMAP,* launched in 2001). These satellites, as well as two balloon experiments, demonstrated that the background radiation is not spread evenly through space, as astronomers thought when it was discovered in 1964. Instead, it shows tiny variations, representing differences in temperature that existed when the radiation first appeared. This "lumpiness" of the background radiation provides information about the shape of space, which in turn depends on the sum of all the mass and energy in the universe. Studies of galaxy clusters have also produced figures that agree with those from the supernova and background radiation research.

All these methods taken together have provided answers to age-old questions that—at least for now—most cosmologists are willing to accept. For instance, the studies agree that the universe is 13 to 14 billion years old. This figure fits with independent measurements of the oldest stars, which appear to be about 12 billion years old.

The combined research also indicates that mass, or matter affected by gravity, makes up about 30 percent of the total matter and energy in the universe. Dark energy, which can also be thought of as some form of matter that is not affected by gravity, accounts for the rest. Baryons, the "heavy" particles forming all the atoms, planets, stars, galaxies, and dust between them, provide only 4 percent of the universe. As Robert Kirshner wrote in his book on supernova research, "We are beginning to paint a new, messy, and wild picture for the cosmos. It's an extravagant universe."

Future Research

As leaders of the groups who made the breakthrough discovery about dark energy, Saul Perlmutter and Brian Schmidt received many honors. Perlmutter won the American Astronomical Society's Henry Chretien Award in 1996, and in 2002, he received the Department of Energy's E. O. Lawrence Award in physics and was elected to the National Academy of Sciences. Schmidt won the Australian government's first Malcolm Macintosh Prize for Achievement in the Physical Sciences in 2000 and the Pawsey Medal, awarded by the Australian Academy of Science, in 2001.

Both men continue to be leaders in astronomical and cosmological research. In addition to supernovas and dark energy, Perlmutter studies pulsars, the dark matter surrounding the Milky Way, and the way matter and gravity bend light. Schmidt's other interests include looking for planets in the solar system beyond Pluto and studying

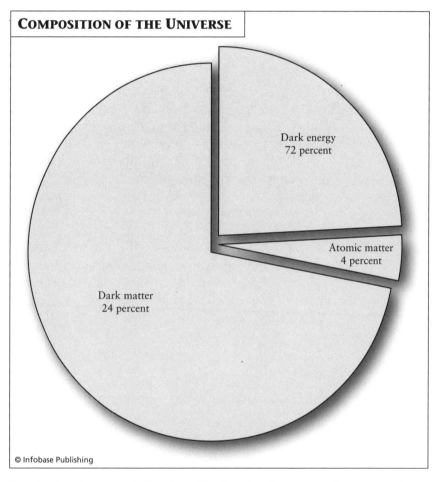

COMPOSITION OF THE UNIVERSE

Dark energy
72 percent

Atomic matter
4 percent

Dark matter
24 percent

© Infobase Publishing

People of ancient times believed that Earth and its human population were the most important things in the universe, but astronomers from Copernicus and Galileo forward have shown that this is not so. Today astronomers and cosmologists believe that all the atoms that make up humans, planets, stars, and galaxies provide a mere 4 percent of the total matter and energy in the universe. Dark matter, perhaps an unknown type of subatomic particles, accounts for another 24 percent. All the rest is dark energy, a mysterious force that opposes gravity.

gamma-ray bursts, which (in an interview for the Australian Academy of Science) he called "the largest explosions in the universe."

Both the Supernova Cosmology Project and the High-Z Supernova Search Team, meanwhile, are seeking new ways to gather and analyze ever-more-distant supernovas. The Supernova Cosmology Project, for instance, has urged the Department of Energy and NASA to build an orbiting optical and near-infrared telescope that the Berkeley team calls SNAP, for SuperNova/Acceleration Probe. Adam Riess, a former High-Z member now at the Space Telescope Science Institute, has established a "Higher-Z Supernova Search Team," which is using the *Hubble Space Telescope*'s Advanced Camera for Surveys to look for very high redshift supernovas. The Berkeley team is working on a similar project.

No Final Answers

Although their research has outlined many features of the universe, both supernova groups agree that in some ways, the cosmos is as mysterious as ever. Important questions about it remain to be answered.

Among the most obvious challenges for future scientists is finding out what dark matter and dark energy really are. Dark matter is likely to consist of one or more kinds of subatomic particles yet to be discovered. Dark energy, a property of empty space itself that grows constantly as the universe expands and more space comes into being, may or may not be Einstein's cosmological constant in a new disguise. It may not be constant at all, but instead change with time.

Continuing supernova research, reaching even farther back in time than the breakthrough discoveries of 1998, suggests that we live in what has been called a "stop-and-go universe." Dark energy is the most important factor in the cosmos today, speeding up its rate of expansion. During the universe's early history, however, matter was more closely packed together than it is now. Theorists have predicted, therefore, that at some time in the past, gravity would have had a greater effect on the expansion rate than dark energy, making the rate of expansion slow down compared to the rate just after the big bang.

If this prediction is true, supernovas from that early era should be brighter than their redshifts would suggest. Near the end of the 1990s, both search groups found a few early supernovas that fit this pattern. They believe that the change from a "stop" universe controlled chiefly by gravity to a "go" universe controlled chiefly by dark energy occurred 5 to 7 billion years ago. They are now trying to identify the changeover point more precisely.

The final fate of the cosmos also remains in doubt. So far, the supernova results suggest that the "runaway" universe will end, not with a bang, or even a gnab, but (as the British poet T. S. Eliot wrote) a whimper. Tens of billions of years from now, the accelerating expansion of space will have pushed galaxies so far apart that light will reach Earth only from other parts of the Milky Way. Eventually, only black holes and burned-out stars will be left—and perhaps ultimately, nothing at all. "That seems to me to be the coldest, most horrible end," Brian Schmidt said in a *Nova* television program in 2000. "It's creepy."

Some cosmologists, however, question whether the accelerating universe must suffer such a "creepy" ending. Paul Steinhardt of Princeton University, for one, claimed in early 2005 that alterations in other dimensions make universes undergo repeated patterns of change in the dimensions that humans can perceive. Steinhardt thinks that the "ripples" found in the cosmic background radiation were caused by material left over from a previous contraction. Someday, he says, a new contraction may begin, eventually starting the cycle of creation over. Future astronomers, perhaps using technology undreamed of today, will have to determine whether Schmidt's, Steinhardt's, or some other theory is correct. As Robert Kirshner put it at the end of his book, *The Extravagant Universe,* "The fun has just begun."

Chronology

1917	Albert Einstein inserts cosmological constant into equations of general relativity
1931	After Edwin Hubble shows that the universe is expanding, Einstein removes the cosmological constant

1959	Saul Perlmutter born in Urbana-Champaign, Illinois
1967	Brian Schmidt born in Montana
1981	Perlmutter graduates from Harvard with B.S. in physics
1980s	Richard Muller develops automated telescope early in the decade
1983	Perlmutter begins doing research at Lawrence Berkeley National Library (LBL) as part of the Berkeley Automated Supernova Search Team
1986	Perlmutter earns Ph.D. from LBL for thesis on automated telescope
1988	With Carl Pennypacker, Perlmutter starts the Supernova Cosmology Project to look for high-redshift type Ia supernovas
1989	Schmidt graduates from University of Arizona with bachelor's degrees in physics and astronomy; Perlmutter becomes sole leader of Supernova Cosmology Project
1992	Supernova Cosmology Project finds its first high-redshift supernova in spring
1993	Schmidt earns Ph.D. from Harvard with thesis on type II supernovas; Robert Kirshner's group at Harvard begins studying type Ia supernovas
1994	Supernova Cosmology Project demonstrates reliability of batch processing
1996	Improvements in analysis convince most astronomers that type Ia supernovas are reliable standard candles
1997	Both supernova groups find that distant supernovas are fainter than expected
1998	Both groups present preliminary results at American Astronomical Society meeting in January; the Supernova Cosmology Project proposes that a new form of energy opposing gravity may exist; Alex Filippenko of the High-Z Supernova Search Group announces in February that the universe's expansion appears to be speeding up; in September, the High-Z group becomes the first to publish its results; late in the year, *Science* chooses the supernova research as the "breakthrough of the year"

1990s	Late in the decade, research teams find evidence that long ago, gravity made the universe's rate of expansion slow down
2000	Brian Schmidt receives Malcolm Macintosh Prize
2002	Saul Perlmutter receives E. O. Lawrence Award and is elected to the National Academy of Sciences
2005	Paul Steinhardt of Princeton suggests that universes expand and contract repeatedly

Further Reading

Books

Anton, Ted. *Bold Science: Seven Scientists Who Are Changing Our World*. New York: W. H. Freeman, 2000.
> Includes a chapter on Perlmutter.

Clark, David H., and F. Richard Stephenson. *The Historical Supernovae*. Oxford: Pergamon Press, 1977.
> Collection of accounts of supernovas observed during historical times, such as those seen in 1054 and 1572.

Goldsmith, Donald. *The Runaway Universe*. Cambridge, Mass.: Perseus Publishing, 2000.
> Describes the discovery of dark energy and how the discovery changed cosmologists' understanding of the universe. Written for a nonscientific audience but is fairly difficult reading.

Kirshner, Robert P. *The Extravagant Universe*. Princeton, N.J.: Princeton University Press, 2002.
> Recounts the development of the High-Z Supernova Search Team and its codiscovery of dark energy. Written for a nonscientific audience but is fairly difficult reading.

Articles

Bartusiak, Marcia. "Beyond the Big Bang: Einstein's Evolving Universe." *National Geographic* 207 (May 2005): 111–120.
> Describes how recent discoveries, including the findings of the supernova teams, have allowed cosmologists to expand on Albert Einstein's

general theory of relativity to describe the beginning and predicted end of the universe.

Heard, Marian. "Interview with Dr. Brian Schmidt." Australian Academy of Science. Available online. URL: http://www.science. org.au/scientists/bs.htm. Posted in 2001. Accessed on April 7, 2005.
> Interview with Schmidt provides extensive background on his life and work.

Hogan, Craig J., Robert P. Kirshner, and Nicholas B. Suntzeff. "Surveying Space-Time with Supernovae." *Scientific American* 280 (January 1999): 46–51.
> Tells how distant supernovas provided evidence that the universe's expansion is accelerating, probably due to energy in space that opposes gravity. Somewhat difficult reading.

Lawrence Berkeley National Laboratory. "Saul Perlmutter Wins E. O. Lawrence Award in Physics." Available online. URL: http://www. lbl.gov/Science-Articles/Archive/Phy-Lawrence-Award-Perlmutter. html. Posted on September 26, 2002. Accessed on April 7, 2005.
> Press release issued when Perlmutter won the award provides background on him and his supernova discoveries.

———. "*Science* Magazine Names Supernova Cosmology Project 'Breakthrough of the Year.' " Available online. URL: http://www. lbl.gov/supernova. Posted on December 17, 1998. Accessed on April 7, 2005.
> Press release describing reactions to the discovery by the Supernova Cosmology Project and the High-Z Supernova Search Team that the universe's expansion is accelerating.

Lemonick, Michael D. "The End." *Time* 157 (June 25, 2001): 48ff.
> Clear account of the supernova teams' 1998 discoveries and later findings, including those about the cosmic background radiation, that fuel speculations about the end of the universe.

Lucas, Thomas, Michael Winship, and Julia Cort. "Runaway Universe." Public Broadcasting System. Available online. URL: http://www.pbs.org/wgbh/nova/transcripts/2713universe.html. Posted on November 21, 2000. Accessed on April 7, 2005.
> Transcript of a *Nova* broadcast in which Brian Schmidt, Robert Kirshner, and other members of the High-Z Supernova Search Team are interviewed and demonstrate their work.

Perlmutter, Saul, et al. "Measurements of Ω and Λ from 42 High-Redshift Supernovae." *Astrophysical Journal* 517 (June 1, 1999): 565–586.

> Scientific paper describing the Supernova Cosmology Project's measurements of the density of the universe (Ω) and the cosmological constant (Λ), based on analysis of 42 distant type Ia supernovas.

———. "Supernovae, Dark Energy, and the Accelerating Universe." *Physics Today* 56 (April 2003): 53–60.

> Difficult but understandable explanation of the discoveries of Lawrence Berkeley National Laboratory's Supernova Cosmology Project, which Perlmutter leads.

Riess, Adam G., et al. "Observational Evidence from Supernovae for an Accelerating Universe and a Cosmological Constant." *Astronomical Journal* 116 (September 1998): 1009–1038.

> Scientific paper reporting the High-Z Supernova Search Team's discovery that the expansion of the universe is speeding up. The group believes that Einstein's cosmological constant, representing an unknown form of energy in deep space, accounts for the increase.

Schmidt, Brian. "The Universe from Beginning to End." Australian Academy of Science. Available online: http://www.science.org. au/sats2004/schmidt.htm. Posted on May 7, 2004. Accessed on April 7, 2005.

> This speech given by Schmidt at an annual "celebration of Australian science" symposium explains the High-Z Supernova Search Team's work and its significance. The speech includes an extensive discussion of related research, for example on the cosmic background radiation, and of the possible nature of dark matter and dark energy.

Web Sites

The High-Z Supernova Search Team. URL: http://cfa-www.harvard.edu/ cfa/oir/Research/supernova/newdata/introduction.html. Accessed on January 31, 2005.

> This group, led by Brian Schmidt, is one of the two teams who discovered that the universe is expanding at an ever-faster rate, fueled by mysterious "dark energy." On the group's Web site, Schmidt presents an exceptionally clear, well-illustrated description of the team's study of type Ia supernovas and the importance of this work in understanding the structure and ultimate fate of the universe. In addition

to explanations, the site includes a list of papers by members of the High-Z team, links to members' home pages, news stories about the team's work, detailed statistics of the group's findings, and descriptions of related projects.

Supernova Cosmology Project. URL: http://supernova.lbl.gov. Accessed on September 26, 2005.

This is the other group studying type Ia supernovas as a way of learning about the past and future of the universe. The group is centered at Lawrence Berkeley National Laboratory and headed by Saul Perlmutter. Its site includes recent results and publications, diagrams and photos, and links.

CHRONOLOGY

1054	A type II supernova appears in the constellation of the Crab; Chinese astronomers describe it, calling it the "guest star"
1543	Nicolaus Copernicus publishes book stating that the Earth goes around the Sun
1572	Tycho Brahe observes a "new star," a type Ia supernova
1609	Galileo Galilei uses a telescope to observe the moons of Jupiter, the phases of Venus, and other astronomical phenomena; Johannes Kepler formulates laws describing the orbits of planets around the Sun
1666	Isaac Newton breaks sunlight into a rainbow, or spectrum, of colored light by passing it through a prism
1781	William Herschel discovers the planet Uranus
1815	Joseph von Fraunhofer invents the spectroscope
1840	Henry Draper takes the first astronomical photograph
1842	Christian Doppler shows that radiation, including sound and light, is shifted higher (to shorter wavelengths) when an object giving off the radiation moves toward an observer and is shifted lower (to longer wavelengths) when the object is moving away
1845	William Parsons, earl of Rosse, builds reflecting telescope nicknamed "the Leviathan"
1846	Johann Gottfried Galle and Heinrich-Louis d'Arrest discover Neptune by checking predictions by John Couch Adams and Urbain-Jean-Joseph La Verrier, based on unexpected features of Uranus's orbit

1859	Gustav Kirchoff and Robert Bunsen show that spectra can be analyzed to reveal the chemical elements in a burning gas, including gases from stars
1860s	James Clerk Maxwell describes electromagnetic radiation and suggests that light is one form of such radiation
1888	Heinrich Hertz produces and detects radio waves and other electromagnetic radiation
1890s	Percival Lowell claims to see canals and vegetation on Mars
1892	On July 6, George Ellery Hale becomes world's first professor of astrophysics
1897	Yerkes Observatory, founded by George Ellery Hale and containing world's largest refracting telescope, dedicated on October 21
1905	George Ellery Hale founds Mount Wilson Observatory
1912	Henrietta Leavitt shows how to use Cepheid variable stars to measure astronomical distances
1915	Albert Einstein publishes general theory of relativity
1917	100-inch (2.5-m) Hooker Telescope goes into service at Mount Wilson Observatory; Einstein adds cosmological constant to relativity theory to explain a universe that does not change
1925	Edwin Hubble announces on January 1 that Andromeda nebula is a galaxy outside the Milky Way
1927	Georges-Henri Lemaître proposes that the universe began with the explosion of a primeval atom
1929	On March 15, Edwin Hubble reports that the universe is expanding
1930s	Fritz Zwicky and Sinclair Smith predict the existence of dark matter
1931	Because of Hubble's discovery, Einstein removes cosmological constant from his equations
1933	Karl Jansky reports in April that the center of the Milky Way appears to be sending out hissing radio static

1937	Grote Reber builds the first radio telescope in his backyard
1946	Lyman Spitzer, Jr., proposes development of a large space telescope and lists its scientific uses
1947–48	George Gamow and Ralph Asher Alpher describe big bang theory and show how atomic nuclei of lightweight elements could have been formed in the first few minutes after the explosion that began the expansion of the universe
1948	On June 3, 200-inch (5-m) telescope at Mount Palomar Observatory dedicated and named Hale Telescope
1949	Ralph Asher Alpher and Robert Herman propose that microwave (radio) radiation released soon after the big bang might be detected
1950	Vera Rubin reports in December that nearby galaxies appear to be rotating around a common center
1951	On March 25, Harold Ewen and Edward Purcell detect 21-centimeter (about 8-in.) hydrogen radiation (radio waves) from the Milky Way
1954	Vera Rubin provides evidence that galaxies are distributed unevenly in space
1957	On October 4, Soviet Union launches first artificial satellite, *Sputnik 1*
1960	Frank Drake conducts Project Ozma, first search for communications from extraterrestrial civilizations, in April and May; Riccardo Giacconi and Bruno Rossi invent the X-ray telescope
1962	On June 18, X-ray detectors discover cosmic background X-radiation and first extrasolar X-ray source
1964	Arno Penzias and Robert Wilson detect cosmic microwave background radiation, providing strong support for the big bang theory
1970	*Uhuru*, first X-ray astronomy satellite, launched on December 12

1970s	Early in the decade, data from *Uhuru* provide first convincing proof of the existence of black holes
1972	Spacecraft *Pioneer 10,* containing engraved message for extraterrestrial civilizations, launched on March 2
1970s	Late in the decade and in the early 1980s, Vera Rubin shows that galaxies are embedded in halos of invisible ("dark") matter with a mass five to 10 times greater than that of the visible galaxies
1978	*Einstein,* first X-ray telescope satellite, launched on November 13
1984	Richard Terrile and Bradford Smith photograph a disk of possible planet-forming material around the star Beta Pictoris; Frank Drake founds SETI Institute, dedicated to search for extraterrestrial intelligence, in November
1990	On April 24, *Hubble Space Telescope* goes into orbit
1995	Michel Mayor and Didier Queloz report discovery of first extrasolar planet in October
1996	Astronomers accept type Ia supernovas as standard candles for measuring distance to faraway galaxies
1998	In January, two research teams announce their conclusion, based on measurements using type Ia supernovas, that the rate of expansion of the universe is increasing because of the effects of "dark energy," a force that opposes gravity
1999	In March, Geoff Marcy and Paul Butler discover first star shown to have multiple planets; *Chandra X-ray Observatory* launched on July 23; on November 7, Marcy and Butler show dimming of starlight caused by a planet passing in front of the star
2000s	Early in the decade, research showing uneven distribution of cosmic background radiation confirms supernova scientists' conclusions about the composition of the universe
2003	*Spitzer Space Telescope,* infrared observatory satellite, launched on August 25
2005	In March, first image of extrasolar planet is made

GLOSSARY

absolute brightness an astronomical object's actual, or true, brightness; if an object's absolute brightness and apparent brightness are both known, its distance from Earth can be determined. *Compare with* APPARENT BRIGHTNESS

Andromeda galaxy (Andromeda nebula) the nearest large galaxy to the Milky Way, located in the constellation Andromeda; known in astronomical catalogs as M31

apparent brightness the seeming brightness of an astronomical object as seen from Earth; apparent brightness varies with the square of the distance. *Compare with* ABSOLUTE BRIGHTNESS.

Arecibo Telescope a radio telescope 1,000 feet (305 m) across, located in a bowl-shaped valley in Arecibo, Puerto Rico, and managed by Cornell University; it is the world's largest single-dish radio telescope

astronomy the science that studies objects beyond Earth's atmosphere and the universe as a whole

astrophysics the branch of science that studies the physical and chemical characteristics of astronomical objects and of matter and energy beyond Earth's atmosphere

barred spiral a type of galaxy with two spiral arms emerging from a long, flat central disk

baryon a massive, strongly interacting subatomic particle; the most common baryons are protons and neutrons

big bang theory the theory that the universe emerged at a specific moment in the past when an infinitely small, infinitely dense point (a singularity) containing all matter and energy suddenly began expanding; the name was given by an opponent of the theory, Fred Hoyle, in 1949. *Compare with* STEADY-STATE THEORY

big crunch   the eventual return to a singularity that would occur if the cosmos contained enough mass for gravity to reverse the universe's expansion

binary star system   two stars orbiting around one another, held together by mutual gravitational attraction

black hole   an object with such a strong gravitational pull that even light cannot escape it

Cepheid variable   a type of very bright star whose light grows and fades in a regular cycle; the longer the cycle, the greater the absolute brightness of the star, a fact that allows Cepheids to be used to measure the distance to larger formations, such as star clusters or galaxies, in which they are embedded

Chandra   a large X-ray telescope satellite launched in 1999; it is named after Indian-born astrophysicist Subrahmanyan Chandrasekhar

charge-coupled device   a computer chip that converts light into electronic signals, allowing images to be formed; it is far more sensitive than photographic film

Copernicus   a satellite, consisting chiefly of a telescope sensitive to ultraviolet light, designed by Lyman Spitzer, Jr., and others and launched in 1972

corona   the very hot outermost layer of a star's atmosphere

coronagraph   a telescope that blocks light from the main body of the Sun or other star so that the faint corona can be observed

Cosmic Background Explorer (COBE)   a satellite designed to observe the cosmic background radiation in infrared and microwave wavelengths; it was launched in 1989

cosmic rays   high-energy subatomic particles that enter Earth's atmosphere from space, traveling at close to the speed of light

cosmological constant   a term, representing a force that opposes gravity, that Albert Einstein added to his equations of general relativity in 1917; he removed it around 1930, but research announced in 1998 suggests that it may exist after all. *See also* DARK ENERGY

cosmology   the study of the origin, structure, and evolution of the universe

dark energy   an unknown form of energy within empty space that opposes gravity and is causing the expansion of the universe to accelerate

dark matter   matter that does not give off light; it makes up 90 to 95 percent of the mass in the universe, and the nature of most of it is unknown

deuterium   a form of hydrogen ("heavy hydrogen") with a nucleus consisting of a proton and a neutron

Doppler shift   a phenomenon discovered by Austrian physicist Christian Doppler in 1842, in which radiation, including sound and light, is shifted higher (to shorter wavelengths) when an object giving off the radiation moves toward an observer and is shifted lower (to longer wavelengths) when the object is moving away

Drake equation   an equation proposed by Frank Drake in 1961 to determine the number of detectable intelligent civilizations in the universe

eccentric orbit   an orbit with an oval rather than a circular shape

Einstein   the first X-ray telescope satellite, launched in 1978

electromagnetic spectrum   the full range of electromagnetic radiation, ranging from gamma rays (with the shortest wavelength, highest frequency, and highest energy) to radio waves (with the longest wavelength, lowest frequency, and lowest energy)

elliptical galaxy   a type of galaxy with an egg-shaped center and no spiral arms

exoplanet   a planet belonging to a star system other than that of the Sun; short for *extrasolar planet*

feed   a secondary antenna in a radio telescope that transmits radio waves focused by the main antenna to a receiver

filled-aperture telescope   a type of radio telescope with a parabolic "dish" main antenna, a secondary antenna, and a receiver

fission reaction   a reaction in which the nuclei of atoms are split

flux density   the strength of a radio signal that falls on a particular area of a detector; it is measured in units called janskys

focus   to concentrate light or other electromagnetic radiation on a single point; also, the point on which radiation is concentrated

fusion reaction   a reaction in which atomic nuclei combine to make a single, heavier nucleus, releasing huge amounts of energy

galaxy   a massive system of millions to trillions of stars and associated gas and dust, rotating about a single center and held together by gravity

gamma rays the form of electromagnetic radiation (photons) with the highest energy and shortest wavelength

gamma-ray bursts the most powerful explosions in the universe, emitting extremely high-energy radiation

gnab gib "big bang" backwards; same as BIG CRUNCH

Hale Telescope the main telescope in the Mount Palomar Observatory, with a mirror 200 inches (5.08 m) across; dedicated in 1948 and named after George Ellery Hale, it was for decades the world's largest single-mirror optical telescope

helium an element first detected in the Sun by spectroscopic analysis in 1868; in 1895, George Ellery Hale showed that it also exists on Earth

Hooker Telescope the chief optical telescope in the Mount Wilson Observatory, with a mirror 100 inches (2.5 m) across; dedicated in 1917, it is named after John D. Hooker, a Los Angeles businessman who donated money for the mirror

Hubble Space Telescope a large space telescope and associated instruments, placed into orbit in 1990 and named after Edwin Hubble

Hubble's law the fact that the distance of astronomical objects from Earth and the speed of their movement, as part of the expansion of the universe, are directly proportional; Edwin Hubble discovered this relationship in 1929

hydrogen the element that is most common, lightest in weight, and first to be created in the universe

image tube a device that, when attached to a spectrograph, enhances images of spectra electronically; Kent Ford invented the combination of image tube and spectrograph in the early 1960s

infrared radiation radiation below the longest wavelength (lowest energy) of visible light but more energetic than microwaves (radio waves)

Infrared Astronomical Satellite (IRAS) a satellite equipped with infrared detectors, launched in 1983

interference radio signals that block or distort reception of other desired signals; also called noise

ionosphere the part of the atmosphere that extends from about 50 to 300 miles above the Earth's surface and contains numerous electrically charged (ionized) atoms

James Webb Space Telescope a successor to the *Hubble Space Telescope,* expected to be launched in 2011, that will collect radiation in the infrared and near-infrared range

Keck telescopes two optical telescopes with mirrors 33 feet (10 m) across, located on Mauna Kea, a dormant volcano in Hawaii

Kepler Space Telescope a space telescope designed to search for extrasolar planets, scheduled to be launched in 2008

large-scale streaming the motion of groups of galaxies toward areas where galaxies are packed more tightly, caused by the gravitational attraction of the densely packed areas

lens a piece of glass or similar material with surfaces curved in a way that allows the lens to gather light and focus it on a point, forming a clear image

light-year a unit for measuring astronomical distances: the distance that light, moving at 186,000 miles (300,000 km), can travel in a year, or about 6 trillion miles (9.5 trillion km)

M31 *see* ANDROMEDA GALAXY

Magellanic Clouds two small galaxies near the Milky Way and the Andromeda galaxy

Milky Way the galaxy in which the solar system is embedded; its center appears as a band of light across the sky in certain latitudes

nebula (pl. nebulae) a cloud of gas and dust in space

neutron star a very small, very dense star created in the supernova explosion of a large star

nova a star that ejects a cloud of gas from its surface in an explosion, becoming temporarily much brighter in the process. *Compare with* SUPERNOVA

nulling interferometry the mixing of two signals in a way that causes them to cancel each other out, allowing weaker signals to be detected

observational cosmology the science of predicting the origin, structure, and evolution of the universe on the basis of astronomical observations

optical telescope a telescope that forms images of astronomical objects by detecting light that comes from the objects

orbit the path that an astronomical object, such as a planet, follows around a larger object, such as a star

parabola   a type of curve, any point of which is equally distant from a fixed point (the focus) and a fixed straight line

parametric amplifier   a form of amplifier that increases the sensitivity of signals while keeping the level of interference (noise) very low

period   the length of time a variable star takes to complete one cycle of brightening and dimming

photometer   a device used to measure the intensity or brightness of light

photon   a unit (quantum or particle) of electromagnetic radiation, especially of light

Pioneers 10 and 11   unmanned spacecraft, launched in 1972 and 1973; they were the first spacecraft intended to leave the solar system and contained plaques with engraved messages for extraterrestrial beings

plasma   a gaslike mass of charged subatomic particles

prism   a triangular or wedge-shaped piece of glass or similar material that breaks up white light into a rainbow (spectrum) of light of different colors

Project Ozma   observation of two nearby stars with a radio telescope, carried out by Frank Drake and his coworkers in April and May 1960; it was the first scientific search for extraterrestrial intelligence

pulsar   a rotating neutron star that sends out pulses of radio waves or other radiation

quantum mechanics   the branch of physics that explains the behavior of subatomic particles; it is based on the idea that energy exists in individual units called quanta

quasar   a distant, starlike object that gives off huge amounts of radio waves and other energy; it may be the nucleus of a galaxy containing a massive black hole

radio astronomy   the branch of astronomy studying astronomical objects that emit radio waves

receiver   a device that amplifies and decodes radio signals sent to it by an antenna

redshift   the Doppler shift toward the red of the spectrum of light sent by an astronomical object moving away from the Earth; the greater an object's redshift, the faster it is moving away and the farther away it is

reflecting telescope (reflector) a telescope that uses a curved mirror or mirrors to gather and focus light

refracting telescope (refractor) a telescope that uses lenses to gather and focus light by bending (refracting) light rays

resolution power to show fine detail and produce sharp images

Rubin-Ford effect movement of the Local Group of galaxies through the universe as a unit; an example of large-scale streaming. *See also* LARGE-SCALE STREAMING

SETI (Search for Extraterrestrial Intelligence) search for communications from extraterrestrial civilizations by examining incoming radio or light radiation for signs of patterns that might have been deliberately placed there

SETI@home software created at the University of California, Berkeley, that allows home computer users to apply their machines' idle processing time to analysis of radio telescope data, looking for signs of possible extraterrestrial communication

SIM PlanetQuest a spacecraft, expected to be launched around 2011, on which several small telescopes will work together to search for extrasolar planets

singularity a point in space-time at which density and gravitational attraction are infinite; the center of a black hole is a singularity, and the big bang theory holds that the universe began expanding from a singularity

solar prominence a huge cloud of glowing gas that erupts from the Sun's surface

sonar (SOund Navigation And Ranging) a method of underwater detection that sends sound waves into water and analyzes the echoes that bounce off objects in the water

spectrogram an image of a spectrum

spectrograph a device that separates light or other electromagnetic radiation into its component wavelengths and records the resulting spectrum

spectroheliograph a device, invented by George Ellery Hale in 1889, that makes an image of the Sun in a single wavelength of light (monochromatic image), corresponding to a single chemical element

spectroscope a device, invented by Joseph von Fraunhofer in 1815, consisting of a spectrograph attached to a telescope; it allows the light of astronomical objects to be spread into spectra for viewing, recording, and analysis

spectrum (pl. spectra) the entire range of wavelengths of light or other electromagnetic radiation, arranged in order of wavelength

spherical aberration a defect in telescopes in which light from the edges of a mirror or lens and light from the center are focused in different places, creating a blurry image

spiral galaxy the most common form of galaxy, consisting of a dense center from which curved arms radiate, creating a spiral shape

Spitzer Space Telescope a telescope satellite that detects radiation in infrared and near-infrared range; it was launched in 2003 and named after Lyman Spitzer, Jr.

standard candles astronomical objects whose absolute brightness is known, allowing their apparent brightness to be used to determine their distance from Earth. Cepheid variables and type Ia supernovas are examples. *See also* ABSOLUTE BRIGHTNESS; APPARENT BRIGHTNESS

steady-state theory a theory, proposed by Fred Hoyle, Arthur Gold, and Hermann Bondi in 1948, that said the universe basically does not change; its expansion is balanced by creation of new matter. *Compare with* BIG BANG THEORY

Stellarator a type of device for containing the plasma necessary for a controlled atomic fusion reaction, developed by Lyman Spitzer, Jr., in 1951

sunspots dark patches on the Sun's surface, which George Ellery Hale showed to be cooler than their surroundings and to contain powerful magnetic fields

supernova (pl. supernovas) gigantic explosions that destroy or nearly destroy stars when the stars' nuclear fuel runs out. Supernovas exist in two types, which have different causes and different spectra. *See also* TYPE IA SUPERNOVA; TYPE II SUPERNOVA

telescope a device that uses either lenses (refracting telescope) or mirrors (reflecting telescope) to gather and focus light or other electromagnetic radiation in a way that magnifies the apparent size of objects and makes them brighter, allowing very distant objects to be observed. *See also* REFLECTING TELESCOPE; REFRACTING TELESCOPE

Terrestrial Planet Finder a space telescope consisting of a coronagraph and a nulling interferometer, expected to be launched in 2020, that will be used to search for small planets that orbit other stars

theory of relativity a theory of motion and energy developed by Albert Einstein in the early 20th century

thermonuclear reaction a reaction, taking place at very high temperatures, in which atomic nuclei fuse to create larger nuclei of different elements, releasing huge amounts of energy in the process

tokamak the most common kind of atomic fusion reactor, first developed in Russia in 1969

transit to pass in front of; used, for example, of a planet passing in front of a star and obscuring a small amount of the star's light

type Ia supernova a type of supernova, all of whose members have similar spectra, allowing it to be used as a standard candle for measuring distances to faraway astronomical objects such as galaxies *See also* STANDARD CANDLES; SUPERNOVA; TYPE II SUPERNOVA

type II supernova a type of supernova that has a different cause and affects different kinds of stars than type Ia supernovas; the spectra of type II supernovas are different enough from one another to keep them from being used as standard candles. *See also* SUPERNOVA; TYPE IA SUPERNOVA

Uhuru the first X-ray detector satellite, launched in 1970

ultraviolet electromagnetic radiation above the shortest wavelength (highest energy) of visible light, but less energetic than gamma rays

very long baseline interferometry a technique in radio astronomy in which observations from widely separated telescopes are recorded and later synchronized and combined into a single signal

Voyagers 1 **and** *2* unmanned spacecraft, launched in 1977, that carried phonographs of voices, sounds, and images from Earth as a message for extraterrestrial civilizations

wavelength one measure of electromagnetic radiation (the other is frequency). Radiation with short wavelengths has greater frequency and higher energy than radiation with long wavelengths.

wide field and planetary camera one of several instruments originally connected to the *Hubble Space Telescope*

Wilkinson Microwave Anisotropy Probe (WMAP) an astronomy satellite, launched in 2001, whose data showed that the cosmic background microwave radiation is not completely evenly distributed in space

X-rays a form of high-energy electromagnetic radiation, discovered by Wilhelm Röntgen in 1895; some astronomical objects are powerful sources of X-rays, and Riccardo Giacconi invented a telescope that collects and focuses this form of radiation

ylem a term used by George Gamow to represent the tremendously hot "soup" of free electrons, protons, neutrons, and radiation that existed just after the big bang

Z a term used to represent the value of an astronomical object's redshift

Zeeman effect a phenomenon that creates divided lines in spectra when the light creating the spectra passes through a strong magnetic field

FURTHER RESOURCES

Books

Bartusiak, Marcia, ed. *Archives of the Universe: A Treasury of Astronomy's Historic Works of Discovery.* New York: Pantheon, 2004.
> Anthology of scientific writings on astronomy from ancient times to the present, with introductions providing explanations and context.

Ferris, Timothy. *Coming of Age in the Milky Way.* New York: William Morrow, 1988.
> Describes humans' historic attempts to learn about the universe in terms of ideas about space, time, and creation.

———, ed. *The World Treasury of Physics, Astronomy, and Mathematics.* Boston: Little, Brown, 1991.
> Anthology of scientific and popular writings has a section on astronomy, which includes writings by Edwin Hubble and Georges-Henri Lemaître.

Lightman, Alan, and Roberta Brawer. *Origins: The Lives and Worlds of Modern Cosmologists.* Cambridge, Mass.: Harvard University Press, 1990.
> Presents long interviews with 27 modern cosmologists and other astronomers, including Vera Rubin, whose research has affected cosmology.

North, John. *The Norton History of Astronomy and Cosmology.* New York: W. W. Norton, 1994.
> Covers astronomy and cosmology around the world from ancient times to the present, with an emphasis on earlier periods. Somewhat difficult reading.

Panek, Richard. *Seeing and Believing.* New York: Viking, 1998.
> History of telescopes from Galileo's day to the development of radio and other telescopes that do not use visible light.

Time-Life editors. *Voyage through the Universe: The New Astronomy.* Alexandria, Va.: Time-Life Books, 1989.
> Well-illustrated account of the development and discoveries of radio telescopes, X-ray telescopes, and observatory satellites.

Todd, Deborah, and Joseph A. Angelo, Jr. *A to Z of Scientists in Space and Astronomy.* New York: Facts On File, 2005.

Biographical encyclopedia provides short profiles of scientists such as George Ellery Hale and Edwin Hubble.

Watson, Fred. *Stargazer: The Life and Times of the Telescope.* New York: Da Capo Press, 2005.

Book by the astronomer in charge of the Anglo-Australian Observatory in New South Wales, Australia, describes the development of astronomy as a science, as well as changes in telescopes.

Zirker, J. B. *An Acre of Glass: A History and Forecast of the Telescope.* Baltimore, Md.: Johns Hopkins University Press, 2005.

Chronicles the development of telescopes, including telescopes that do not use visible light and satellite telescopes, as well as the work of pioneer astronomers.

Internet Resources

AbsoluteAstronomy.com. Available online. URL: http://www.absoluteastronomy.com. Accessed on May 2, 2005.

Provides quick facts on planets, moons, constellations, stars, Messier objects, nebulas, and galaxies.

Amazing Space. Space Telescope Science Institute's Office of Public Outreach. Available online. URL: http://amazing-space.stsci.edu. Accessed on February 4, 2005.

Educational site includes online explorations, news, links, and homework help related to the *Hubble Space Telescope.*

Astronomy for Kids "and Supervised Adults." Dustbunny.com Available online. URL: http://www.dustbunny.com/afk. Accessed on May 2, 2005.

Site for young people covers sky maps, planets, sky wonders, constellations, information for beginners in astronomy, and "postcard" images of spectacular astronomical objects.

HubbleSite.org Hubble Space Telescope Web site. Available online. URL: http://hubblesite.org. Accessed on February 4, 2005.

Includes a news center, a gallery, information about *Hubble*'s discoveries, illustrated descriptions of how the telescope and its instruments work, interactive games and activities for students, and reference information about the telescope.

KidsAstronomy.com. Available online. URL: http://www.kidsastronomy.com. Accessed on May 2, 2005.

Site for young people supplies astronomy-related games, a dictionary, a teacher's corner, free online classes, news, and background information on various astronomical topics.

National Aeronautics and Space Administration (NASA) Web site. Available online. URL: http://www.nasa.gov. Accessed on September 26, 2005.
> Supplies material for children, students, educators, media and press, researchers, industry, and employees. Site covers NASA facts and history, news and events, multimedia, and missions.

Physlink.com. Physics and Astronomy online. Available online. URL: http://www.physlink.com. Accessed on May 2, 2005.
> Site covers news stories involving both astronomy and physics, as well as links to education, resources, and other information. College level.

PlanetQuest. California Institute of Technology and National Aeronautics and Space Administration. Available online. URL: http://planetquest.jpl.nasa.gov. Accessed on January 31, 2005.
> Site devoted to the search for extrasolar planets contains material for educators, scientists, and the press, including news, a multimedia gallery, an atlas of planets discovered so far, and links.

Space.com. Available online. URL: http://www.space.com. Accessed on May 2, 2005.
> Includes space news, astronomical images, and science, technology, and entertainment related to space and astronomy.

Space Telescope Science Institute (STScI). Available online. URL: http://www.stsci.edu. Accessed on September 26, 2005.
> Site provides information on the *Hubble Space Telescope (HST),* the forthcoming *James Webb Space Telescope,* scientific projects involving the *HST,* astronomical catalogs and surveys, community missions, and data archives, including an extensive image collection.

What Is Radio Astronomy? National Radio Astronomy Observatory. Available online. URL: http://www.nrao.edu/whatisra. Accessed on September 26, 2005.
> Describes the science and history of radio astronomy, including how radio telescopes work and profiles of pioneers such as Karl Jansky and Grote Reber.

Periodicals

Amateur Astronomy Magazine
Published by Tom Clark
5450 Northwest 52 Court
Chiefland, FL 32626
Telephone: (352) 490-9101
http://www.amateurastronomy.com
> Focuses on amateur astronomy, including observing and telescope making.

Astronomical Journal
Published by the University of Chicago Press for the American
Astronomical Society
John S. Gallagher III

Astronomical Journal
Space Astronomy Lab, Chamberlin Hall
University of Wisconsin
1150 University Avenue
Madison, WI 53706
Telephone: (608) 265-6005
http://www.journals.uchicago.edu/AJ
   Scientific journal founded in 1849 stresses observational research and
features such subjects as quasars and supernovas.

Astronomy
Published by Kalmbach Publishing Co.
21027 Crossroads Circle
P.O. Box 1612
Waukesha, WI 53187-1612
Telephone: (800) 533-6644
http://www.astronomy.com
   Popular magazine describes astronomy and space news, star charts,
space missions, and background information.

Astrophysical Journal
Published by University of Chicago Press for the American
Astronomical Society
Steward Observatory
University of Arizona
933 North Cherry Avenue
Tucson, AZ 85721
Telephone: (520) 621-5145
http://www.journals.uchicago.edu/ApJ
   Premier scientific journal in the field, founded by George Ellery Hale in
1895. Includes supplements providing background on recent discoveries.

Mercury
Published by the Astronomical Society of the Pacific
390 Ashton Avenue
San Francisco, CA 94112
Telephone: (415) 337-1100
http://www.astrosociety.org/pubs/mercury/mercury.html
Showcases the latest developments in astronomy and monthly sky events. Sometimes includes profiles of astronomers.

Sky and Telescope
Published by Sky Publishing Corp.
49 Bay State Road
Cambridge, MA 02138-1200
Telephone: (800) 253-0245
http://skyandtelescope.com
Popular magazine describes recent news in the field, monthly views of the sky, tips on observing, and background information.

Societies and Organizations

American Astronomical Society (http://www.aas.org) 2000 Florida Avenue NW, Suite 400, Washington, DC 20009-1231. Telephone: (202) 328-2010.

American Association of Amateur Astronomers (http://www.astromax.com) P.O. Box 7981, Dallas, TX 75209-7981.

Astronomical Society of the Pacific (http://www.astrosociety.org) 390 Ashton Avenue, San Francisco, CA 94112. Telephone: (415) 337-1100.

The Planetary Society (http://www.planetary.org) 65 North Catalina Avenue, Pasadena, CA 91108. Telephone: (626) 793-5100.

Royal Astronomical Society (http://www.ras.org.uk) Burlington House, Piccadilly, London W1J 0BQ, United Kingdom. Telephone: (020) 7734-4582.

INDEX